Low-Demand Parenting

of related interest

Parenting Rewired
How to Raise a Happy Autistic Child in a Very Neurotypical World
Danielle Punter and Charlotte Chaney
ISBN 978 1 83997 072 6
eISBN 978 1 83997 073 3

The Complete Guide to Therapeutic Parenting
A Helpful Guide to the Theory, Research and What it Means for Everyday Life
Jane Mitchell and Sarah Naish
ISBN 978 1 78775 376 1
eISBN 978 1 78775 377 8

The Family Experience of PDA
An Illustrated Guide to Pathological Demand Avoidance
Eliza Fricker
ISBN 978 1 78775 677 9
eISBN 978 1 78775 678 6

Low-Demand Parenting

Dropping Demands, Restoring Calm, and Finding Connection with your Uniquely Wired Child

Amanda Diekman

Jessica Kingsley Publishers
London and Philadelphia

First published in Great Britain in 2023 by Jessica Kingsley Publishers
An imprint of John Murray Press

1

Copyright © Amanda Diekman 2023

The right of Amanda Diekman to be identified as the Author
of the Work has been asserted by her in accordance with
the Copyright, Designs and Patents Act 1988.

Front cover image source: Shutterstock®.

A CIP catalogue record for this title is available from the
British Library and the Library of Congress

ISBN 978 1 83997 768 8
eISBN 978 1 83997 769 5

Printed and bound in Great Britain by Clays Ltd

Jessica Kingsley Publishers' policy is to use papers that are natural,
renewable and recyclable products and made from wood grown in
sustainable forests. The logging and manufacturing processes are expected
to conform to the environmental regulations of the country of origin.

Jessica Kingsley Publishers
Carmelite House
50 Victoria Embankment
London EC4Y 0DZ

www.jkp.com

John Murray Press
Part of Hodder & Stoughton Limited
An Hachette UK Company

For the greatest teachers, my three children,
who have taught me everything I know.
May you know your deep why, may you trust
yourselves, and may our love always lead you home.

Contents

Chapter One

My Story

I had three boys in four years, each of them with their own cluster of uniqueness, personality, diagnoses, and neurological differences. We are a proudly neurodiverse family, as well as a mixed neurology family, and together we have created a vibrant low-demand family culture. But it has not always been easy.

Before I became a parent, I was pretty confident I'd be a good one. When my first son was born, I was so endlessly in love with him that I couldn't sleep. Exhausted, I would lie awake watching him breathe, admiring the tiny faces he made in slumber, awash in the reverie of new motherhood.

When I gave birth to my third son in four years, I was still hopelessly in love with my children, but parenthood was killing me. My oldest son Owen changed his clothes dozens of times each day, banged his head on walls, and faked injuries. Our house filled with his screams, as he seemed to struggle with every transition of every day. We balanced on the head of a pin, trying to get it right every time to prevent a catastrophic meltdown. I could not carry on with my life as it was. I left my job and dedicated myself to figuring out what was happening in my family. Every aspect of our parenting life was so incredibly difficult, and I had no reference point because if anything my second child Michael was more difficult than my first. He was a ball of rage, a ticking time bomb, and we never knew what would set him off. The triggers were endless. In his dysregulated state, he was like a wild animal, desperate to destroy in order to survive. He ripped apart books that we placed in his crib, he destroyed his toys. The play therapist commented that four-year-old Owen seemed terrified of his younger brother.

At two, Michael came out of his silent shell one day by unexpectedly yelling "my die you!" at kids on the playground, pushing them and biting them without provocation. From then on, I perpetually hovered a hands-length away to keep other children safe from his uncontrolled aggression. He would bend down to kiss my new-born Leo and then punch him in the face. My bedrock assumption that I was a good parent was on extremely shaky ground. The daily challenges pushed my nervous system beyond its breaking point. The deep waters of postpartum depression rose up, and I was drowning.

My children's meltdowns focused intensely on me. I was covered in bruises. We had a few near misses where someone almost got really hurt. A permanent jagged scar on one child's eyelid is a daily reminder of just how close that rock came. My body was so tense it hurt. My muscles ached when I finally laid down at night. I tried progressive muscle relaxation by tensing and releasing muscles, a technique I read about on the internet and decided to try. But tensing up my muscles was so familiar from surviving all the day's disasters that it made me weep. Tears like a winter rain, a steady all-day rain, interminable, miserable. I never got to the relaxation part. I just fell into pieces.

I tried to talk to other parents about what I was facing: "It's really hard to get your kids dressed, right?" I would casually ask, desperate for someone whose story reflected mine. "Yeah," they would say with a shrug, "kids can be so picky." "So does it take you an hour to get them dressed? Do they have elaborate rituals to tie their shoes? Do they hit you, scream in your face? Are you walking on eggshells all the time?" Startled, blank faces stared back at me, as heads slowly shook. "No, no, it's not like that for us. You should see a therapist."

When we started therapy, if anything it got worse. The psychologist proposed a more rigid set of expectations, rewards, and punishments. When I calmly, lovingly shared this plan, my four-year-old turned to his younger brother. "Come on, let's get her," he said and the two of them attacked. They punched and scratched me as I sacrificed myself to protect the baby, and then they ran out the front door, slamming it behind them. I dissolved into tears. *That is not how it was supposed to go. I'm getting this all wrong. Why is this happening?*

Desperate for solutions, I turned to parenting books to guide me. One of my parenting gurus made me believe that holding boundaries with kids is the most important thing. I found myself holding firm to all kinds of bizarre things that I said but didn't mean: "I told you if you didn't keep two hands on the grocery cart, I would put back those Oreos." "If you even look at your brother, we're leaving!"

I began to even annoy myself with my rules and expectations, and I was drowning in follow-through. My children observed and latched on to my obsession with consistency. They began pointing out each rule that another broke and insisting on punishment.

Our family culture became warped around this oppressive cause-and-effect parenting. We were all trapped. My middle child, Michael, began to say, "Fine, kick me out of the family!" to show me that no matter what punishment I sent his way, he would not care. He would not bend.

I looked in the mirror and did not recognize this person, a familiar experience. I had always struggled with masks, camouflaging like a chameleon. For nearly four decades I wanted nothing more than to be normal. I blurred any harsh edges of my personality, ceased having opinions, and cultivated all my most universally likable traits to ensure that the largest number of people would like me at all times.

It was exhausting to be so likable all the time. I held myself to the highest standards and never let myself off the hook. The punishment for breaking a social rule was the pain of feeling "different," so I was a careful critic of my own abnormality.

I will be liked. I will be safe. No one can hurt me if I do not have any "me" to be hurt.

I held boundaries everywhere, with my kids, with myself. I never ceased playing the part. For 38 years, I believed that this universally likable mask was my Self, and that the immense effort it took to play that part was simply my fault. Not knowing what it felt like to inhabit anyone else's skin, I assumed that others were trying just as hard, but made it look easier. They played their parts and did it better. I was simply not coping well with the reality of being human.

I re-read my parenting books, looking for the places where they admit that sometimes, even when you do your best, these strategies don't work as planned. I kept searching for the sections where they described kids who don't fit the paradigm, or gave me a template for finding my way back to their Right Path from the deep, dark, scary woods on either side where we seemed to have stumbled. But no, the system doesn't fail. The parents fail. The parents fail to implement the system properly. This was what my parenting gurus led me to believe—I have failed. I am alone in the dark. My fear grew. We were off the path, and no one seemed to see us. The gurus kept insisting that if I was just consistent enough, if I tried hard enough, if I didn't give in, then my kids would be ok, that we could have a future of joy and success.

I dreamt of this happy future all the time, the day when I finally got it right and we would experience the calm and ease that other families seemingly accessed all the time. I dreamt of quiet crafting projects that ended in lovely creations that made us all proud— instead of ending with creations ripped into tiny pieces and the sounds of screams echoing around the house.

I dreamt of family meals where everyone shared something that happened in their day, full of warm connection over lovingly pre-pared food, a ritual that eased us into the drowsy connection of cosy bedtimes. Each night, I expected my fantasy not the reality of our dinners, when the smell of my lovingly prepared food sent one child under the table, making gagging and retching noises like a cat with a hairball. I never seemed to expect the pervasive inability to put both bottom cheeks on the chair, the cups knocked over onto plates with chicken nuggets now swimming in water and a devastated child demanding new ones right away and extra crispy.

I dreamt of a time when every day might not feel so hard. It shimmered beyond my reach, tantalizing in its promise of peace. If I followed the steps and stayed on the path, we would get there. And once I got there, I could rest. I was a woman chasing a dream that never arrived.

I did not see my parenting story reflected anywhere, so in my mind, we were the only ones failing. The kids were too wild to attend most social gatherings, and I was too tired to care. Disconnection haunted every corner of my life. I struggled to sleep. Nightmares came like ocean waves, crashing endlessly, some mild and others so violent they slammed me to the ground, disoriented and sore. Despite the cool winter air, I would sweat through my clothes.

At the heart of the pandemic, after trying four different school settings over the course of four months, my son Michael went into what we now know was autistic burnout. He watched YouTube for 12 hours a day, alone in his room under a blanket, eating processed crunchy snacks. He did not look at me or speak to me. He was furious—an active volcano, either silent and rumbling or spewing hot lava.

My heart ached for connection with my son, and I was terrified. I didn't know about autistic burnout yet. We hadn't even heard the term "low-demand parenting." All I knew is that he was suffering deeply. I knew that isolation and endless screen-time were not signs of health for a six-year-old. And at the same time, we got to this point because I pushed and pushed. What would happen if I released instead? What would happen if I trusted that this too had a role to play?

I always knew that this child was very different from his peers, that we had a zebra in a world of horses. When I handed over the completed autism screening to the nurse at his two-year-old check-up, I nearly ran into the hallway to call her back. "You're not asking me the right questions!" I wanted to say. "I've got boxes to check! My child checks boxes!" But I doubted and blamed myself, suppressing the power of my intuition, and I said nothing.

Several years later, at the end of an occupational therapy appointment, I summoned up my courage and stumbled through asking his therapist if we should pursue an autism evaluation for Michael. I brought up his mix of sensory sensitivity, difficulty communicating, intense interests, and emotional dysregulation. She downplayed my concerns using flawed and outdated knowledge of autism. "He is empathetic and feels deeply. You have nothing to worry about." I wanted to correct her: I wasn't worried; I was hopeful. I was desperate for some expert, some guru to say, "Yes, we've seen this before. Yes, you're right. You can trust this intuition." It didn't feel right, but I believed her. Another tiny dream died. A dream that there might be a name for a kid like mine. A dream that there was a community out there who would understand. A dream that Michael needed something different than the world around him because he was a world unto himself.

For the first six years of Michael's life, I leaned on the traditional parenting paradigm and pored over the same volumes as everyone else, desperate to find a way to bring calm and normalcy to our out-of-control family life. I began to call these parenting experts my "choir" because they sang together around certain themes: *Kids need boundaries. You are the adult; you must be in control. When kids misbehave, it's because the parents are messing up. You have to stay calm, because calm, connected parents have kind, gentle kids.*

These books filled me up with "shoulds"—all the things I should be doing to be a good parent, to wrangle my zebra into a bit and saddle like all the other horses. And it wasn't just the books. The parenting culture all around me seemed happy to fill in the gaps with judgment, side eye, and casual commentary about some other parent who was too permissive, whose kids ran all over her, and who needed to get control of her children.

Fuelled by desperation, I began to investigate my son's possible neurodivergence. I made lists. A notebook filled with lists, lists of lists. Every page had one of the *Diagnostic and Statistical Manual of Mental Disorders* criteria for diagnosing autism written at the top and listed below were the pieces of evidence. Except instead of being examples from my son's life, they were examples from mine. My research brought me to the inescapable opinion that I might be autistic. I was terrified because I was discovering just how desperately I *wanted* to be autistic. My terror was not of this new label. I was terrified that I would lose another way to belong. I was desperate not to fail at being this type of human too.

In the summer of 2021, just a few months apart, my son and I were both diagnosed with autism. Michael received his diagnosis from cold and clinical Duke University Autism Center complete with one-way mirrors and endless forms, and four months later, I got my diagnosis over Zoom from a perky and fidgety middle-aged woman who is autistic and ADHD herself, complete with nervous laughter, rambling answers, and a deep kinship.

When I looked at myself in the mirror, a new self blinked at me, freshly awakened, bleary in the bright light of day. An autistic self, filled with self-knowledge, dreaming new dreams. Dreaming of letting it all go.

It felt like a miracle, this brand new thought: *Am I allowed to let things go? I don't have to worship at the altar of consistency and desperately fear the evil of being permissive? What about all my other gurus who say that kids are always testing boundaries and need their grown-ups to hold firm so they can feel safe? Admittedly this strategy is failing spectacularly in our case.* This was the first time that I wondered whether it was my strategy failing, and not me.

Suddenly, I had new eyes to see these failings and failures. Our life had been falling apart, but I wondered if those words were true. Something was falling apart. The pandemic stripped away some; our present reality stripped away much more. The touchstones that told me we were ok failed and fell away. But if life wasn't falling apart, what was?

I joined an online support group of other parents whose children were anxious and explosive like mine. I recognized myself and my kids in so many stories. I was told over and over that it was good that I was asking these questions while they are still young. I was assured that there was plenty of time to change, that it is never too late. I got pictures of where this path would lead if I did not get out of the way, if I continued to insist and enforce and draw boundaries that kept us trapped rather than leading us out of this maze. More than anything, I received the self-compassionate message that kids are doing their best with what they have, and so are their adults. We do not escape the maze for our kids alone. Our own liberation is bound up in theirs.

In this support group, I first heard the words "Pathological Demand Avoidance" (PDA), a little-known profile of autism. The first time I read the words "PDA is an anxiety-driven need to remain in control," I felt my stomach drop. I stayed up way too late absorbing every drop of information I could find. This was real. This had a name. At last, I found a community that could help me see, understand, and connect with my suffering son. PDA is a neurobiological condition that wires with an extreme and pervasive need for autonomy and control. Any perceived threats to that freedom produce a panic-driven anxiety reaction. PDAers will fight, flee, faint, or fawn as if their lives literally depend on it.

Diagnosing and identifying PDA in children is a complex challenge, as it is not yet included in the Diagnostic and Statistical Manual of Mental Disorders (DSM-5-TR),[1] which is used by clinicians to diagnose accurately in the United States and is used as a gold standard around the world. In the United Kingdom, PDA can be identified as a part of the autism diagnostic process, according to their NICE Guidelines,[2] which include demand avoidance as a criterion of autism. The National Autistic Society in the UK has issued detailed profiles for PDA and diagnostic criteria to aid clinicians. Because of the challenges with identification, rigorous studies are also lacking. That said, PDA adults have engaged in tremendous advocacy and training, enabling parents and clinicians to get the best possible data—that of lived experience.

Like a child who has experienced complex trauma, PDAers have a hair-trigger nervous system. They explode without warning to the ordinary demands of everyday life. In order to heal and thrive, many PDAers require a low-demand parenting approach, including releasing tiny, subtle demands like responding to a question with words, or eating at a certain time. My son Michael was one of those kids. He needed me to release all the other parenting methods I relied on and to root out all the false ideas that lurked beneath. He needed radical trust and acceptance, so that I could show up wholeheartedly in the low-demand lifestyle he required.

I began by telling my children, "I think I've made a mistake. I don't think rewards and punishments actually work for you. I think you are doing your best all the time." I nodded along with my own words. *I am doing my best, all the time.*

I looked at my suffering child, and I finally felt free from all the shoulds that screamed in my ears that good parents don't give endless screen-time and good parents don't feed processed food and good parents don't have children who rip up all the books on their

---

1   American Psychiatric Association, *Diagnostic and Statistical Manual of Mental Disorders (DSM-5-TR)*. Washington DC: APA, 2022.

2   National Institute for Health and Care Excellence, *Autism spectrum disorder in under 19s: recognition, referral and diagnosis* (NICE guideline CG128). London: NICE, 2017. https://www.nice.org.uk/guidance/cg128/resources/autism-spectrum-disorder-in-under-19s-recognition-referral-and-diagnosis-pdf-35109456621253.

bookshelf. I was beginning to trust my child more than the chorus of judgmental parenting experts that endlessly sang in my ears. I wanted to trust him enough to let him heal in his own way and to follow his own instincts. His PDA body and brain would lead him toward what he needed to regulate, to rebuild, and to heal. Whether it was the standard approach or not, it was what he needed. I trusted that this too was good, that this too was right, and that this too would lead him forward on his unique life's journey.

Trust also meant honing my own parenting instincts, learning to listen to my own wise inner voice, instead of the many other voices that clamor to tell me what to do. Finding inner wisdom and intuition is a crucial part of the story. As I accepted my true self, I unfolded in trust for my children.

One of the fiercest tethers that kept me locked to the mainstream path was my fear of being a "bad mom." I so, so, so badly wanted to be good. I was raised by a neurodivergent mother, and I saw the judgment and shame heaped on her in the 1980s in a conservative culture that saw any deviation from the norm as a violation of the code of good motherhood. Deep inside, I nestled a kernel of commitment—I would never step off the path and be shamed as she was. Sadly, that very conviction kept me locked in cycles of fear, blame, and shame that nearly led me into total breakdown.

Acceptance moves like a dance in families, a swirl of mutuality. But the true transformation of radical acceptance started with accepting myself. As I learned to see my life through the eyes of neurodiversity—not broken or wrong, but different and good—I gained eyes to see my children as they are. As I accepted my own limits, needs, and disabilities, I accepted my children, limited, needy, and struggling in a world not built for them.

And as I practice loving kindness toward myself, as I radically accept my limits and needs, I am remaking the world for my children.

Our little world, which, it turns out, is their whole world.

Our struggling children need us to trust them. They need us to see them. They need us to release our projections and expectations and the hopes and dreams we've held onto. They need us to accept them, right where they are. Low-demand parenting requires radical acceptance. It says to the kid right in front of you: I see you, just as you are. I will release all the projections, shoulds, hopes, and dreams I've held tightly to. I will let go of all the plans I've made for you. And instead, I will see where you are, right now, and accept that this is an ok place to be. You are ok here. I love you right here.

Even when that "right here" is a radical low point.

Maybe life doesn't need to feel so hard. Maybe we are delicately calibrated machinery trying to navigate a world not built for us. Maybe we all need to let each other off the hook.

When my child said, "No, I won't do it!" I began to say, "Ok!" I slowed down enough to decide if that thing really mattered to me at all, and if it didn't, I dropped it. After all, I'm creating a new world.

The rules I played by for 38 years didn't need to bind me anymore. They never made me feel alive. They weren't written for me. And it's my job to rewrite the story so my children get to thrive, starting with our little family, our world.

I used to believe that kids desperately need to know that adults are in charge, and that if I wavered or backed down, I would do irreparable harm. Now I believe that kids desperately need to know that their adults are with them, that we see and honor their effort, and that we can change for them. Now I let my children off the hook all the time, and in their eyes I see myself without a mask. Unafraid to break the rules. Unconcerned about being liked. Because I like the woman I see through their eyes—a strong and courageous mother who will transform the world for them.

To stand with your child, just as they are, in radical acceptance, is one of the hardest things a parent can do.

OUR FIRST SUCCESS

As we started to move down the path of radical acceptance, I saw Michael's struggle to communicate clearly with us. Mouth words were hard; they got stuck inside my sweet young one who wanted desperately to express his needs but could not. He raged and screamed instead, allowing this powerful communication to flow through his body and into the world. Like many PDAers, he was fully verbal and precociously social, but when he felt threatened or demands piled up, words would drop out completely. I saw that mouth words were not his primary language. Instead, his body would do his talking for him. I began to see the rages as a part of his resilience, his fierce determination to be known. He would not play small in the world. *Hallelujah,* I whispered.

To ease the challenge of expression, I made communication boards for the toughest times of day and the hardest situations for him to talk. Mornings were always hard, so I printed out pictures of his favorite breakfasts and laminated it. I discovered a boundless passion for laminating. Michael could point, or on days when that was too hard, put a favorite toy on top of his choice. Food was then delivered for him to eat on his own, in silence with his tablet. No mouth words required but loads of communication achieved. We discovered this formula for calm mornings the hard way—by removing every piece of the breakfast experience that was hard for him until we landed on what worked. When my expectation consistently matched my boy's capacity, we'd arrived. Was this the way happy families in movies eat breakfast? No. Was this how I imagined it would be to start the day in vibrant connection with my son? No. Did it make us happy, give us deep connection, and start our day right? YES.

Some days even the picture board was too much. The experience of hunger is an internal demand and produces anxious resistance in my boy. He raged against this pressure to fuel his body, but then the hunger fuelled more rages. We landed on a food combination that he would nearly always accept—pretzels and Nutella. This favorite food combo eased the demand, was exceedingly familiar, a total pleasure. We now buy Nutella in bulk and release the shame that this dessert is now our child's most eaten nutritional item. It is working, and we accept it.

I created a laminated choice board for restoration after a meltdown. In the lead up to a meltdown, there was no rationalizing, no choosing, no connecting. In the moment of meltdown, I simply kept people as safe as I could. But in the aftermath, I slid in a choice board with pictures of him doing his most calming nurturing activities—wrestling dad, snuggling mom, being alone, watching his tablet, eating crunchy snacks. On our good days, I could begin to see patterns and to anticipate meltdowns. At tricky times of day, I slid this choice board next to him without saying anything, and it would sit there like a safety net, ready to catch us if we fell.

These laminated papers soon looked battered from so many times smashed, folded, crumpled and thrown. They looked like they'd been through battle. I looked better. My eyes began to sparkle; my shoulders rose up. We'd figured something out, and this unlocking swept gratitude and hope into my heart.

Ever so gradually, almost imperceptibly, Michael healed. We rediscovered one another, like wild animals exploring spring after a long hibernation. We would sit in silence, a gentle touch connecting us, fingers interlaced, and eventually words followed. I brought him a bowl of pretzels and set them down silently. He looked up, smiled, and chirped, "Thanks mom!" I walked back to my room where I buried my face in my hands and wept with gratitude. I was grateful for every healing glance, every hug, every giggle. As square pegs, we know the world is filled with round holes, but our home doesn't need to be one. This boy and I begin to explore the corners, carving out a square home where we can all belong.

Soon, a day passed without any meltdowns. Michael's occupational therapist's face glowed when she told me of a challenge that Michael managed smoothly in session, and she lowered her voice, "He's doing so well! You should be proud." And I was proud. Mornings remained the most challenging part of the day, but one morning, Michael looked up at me and requested cereal calmly with words, as though he did it that way every morning. I controlled my shocked face and delivered his food in silence, still afraid to bring my own voice into the interaction. He ate breakfast under his blanket like usual and emerged asking me to play. It was a turning point day, a pivot day, a before-and-after day. Days of watching YouTube for 12 hours were over. Kicking and banging on locked doors went down. His eyes sparkled again, and his creativity began to explode. He invented endless creatures out of pipe cleaners and built elaborate 3D structures out of Lego, talking all the while, talking, talking, talking.

In this new season, he began talking enough to make up for the months and months of silence. He had something to say and he needed me to listen. This new child was distinctively autistic, no longer hiding his uniqueness nor his struggles. Before, he would be dramatically different in public than he was in home. In this new season, he began to be more or less the same. If he was running, he would flap his hands up and down, up and down, like a tiny flying bird that cannot quite lift off. If he couldn't do anything besides scream in my face, he would do it, regardless of the situation. If he needed to chew, he would use his chewie, without fear of who might be watching. In his darkest burnout, I thought it would never end. But now, he played and wiggled and crashed and jumped most of his hours, and I watched, amazed. When did the healing happen? I was watching the whole time. Did I miss it? Perhaps he walked his own path too. Perhaps he had been growing all along.

I do not need gurus anymore to tell me how to connect with my child. No expert chorus deafens my hearing or blocks my inner voice. The days of shaming myself for getting it wrong, for being wrong, are over. I have hard-won confidence that I know my child, that he knows himself, and that connection and trust are the core of all good parenting. Now I believe that it is good to step off the Right Path and explore the woods for a while.

Low-demand parenting means stepping off the established path and risking being called "permissive" or "lax." People will judge. People will misunderstand. But it is an act of radical love and acceptance. Low-demand parenting is a movement of grace toward a suffering child.

As my sons and I walk this path together, hand in hand, I eventually realize that my children are in the lead, confidently walking their own way, while I walk behind, beaming. I proudly follow my kids. I don't need to be in the lead. Trust means stumbling, falling, getting back up. It means being willing to make mistakes and learn from them. Trust means giving them enough room to be creative and to dream their own dreams. I trust the spirit that leads them, as surely as it leads me.

None of us need gurus to shape a good life. All we need is one another.

Chapter Two

The Neuroscience of Connection

THE DOMINANT PARADIGM: PUNISHMENT AND REWARD PARENTING

Contrary to popular belief and common parenting practice, children are hardwired to please their adults, and do not lack motivation to do the right thing.

This is a fairly radical belief in modern culture, but it is supported by cutting edge brain science[1] and leading psychologists.[2] However, the implications are massive.

The basic assumption underlying punishment and reward parenting is that kids need to be incentivized to do the right thing, because the primary thing they lack is motivation and self-control,

---

1 "Brain science," Stephen Porges, *The Polyvagel Theory: Neurophysiological Foundations of Emotions, Attachment, Communication, and Self-Regulation.* New York: W. W. Norton, 2011. Stephen Porges, *The Pocket Guide to the Polyvagel Theory: The Transformative Power of Feeling Safe.* New York: W. W. Norton, 2017. Brain science adapted to therapeutic models in Deb Dana, *The Polyvagel Theory in Therapy: Engaging the Rhythms of Regulation.* New York: W. W. Norton, 2018.
2 "Leading psychologists": "The three pathways and the check-in," Mona Delahooke, *Brain-Body Parenting: How to Stop Managing Behavior and Start Raising Joyful, Resilient Kids.* New York: HarperCollins, 2022, p.80. "Key themes: kids do well if they can, your child would prefer to be doing well," Ross W. Greene, *Raising Human Beings: Creating a Collaborative Partnership with your Child.* New York: Scribner, 2016, pp.38–39. "Co-regulation," Stuart Shanker, *Self-Reg: How to Help Your Child (and You) Break the Stress Cycle and Successfully Engage with Life.* New York: Penguin, 2016.

and that any number of rewards or punishments can be used to influence behavior toward the desired results.[3]

Sometimes these rewards and punishments are straightforward like time out, sticker charts and prize boxes. Other times they are more subtle like parental approval or disappointment, parental energy, or parental attention. Have you ever been worried that by listening and paying attention to your child's meltdown, you will encourage this behavior? Have you been told that by "giving in" you will reinforce that this is a good way to get what they want?

Dr. Ross Greene, in his 1998 book *The Explosive Child*, popularized a radical new theory—that kids do well when they can, not only when they want to.[4] He points out that the traditional parenting approach makes it parents' job to teach "self-control" by making it more pleasant to do what parents want and less pleasant to do what parents don't want.

However, brain science shows that children actually need parents who stay attuned and connected through all their challenging behaviors and powerful emotions, that having a connected adult is the most essential factor in children's long-term health and positive development.[5]

The most important thing a parent can do when children are having a hard time is stay connected.

Disapproval, disappointment, dismissal, ignoring—all are associated with negative outcomes for children and can be mapped in brain science.[6] The heart of this science comes from a subconscious practice called co-regulation.[7]

---

3   Alfie Kohn, *Punished by Rewards: The Trouble with Gold Stars, Incentive Plans, A's, Praise, and Other Bribes.* New York: Houghton Mifflin, 1999.

4   Ross Greene, *The Explosive Child: A New Approach for Understanding and Parenting Easily Frustrated, Chronically Inflexible Children.* New York: HarperCollins, 1998.

5   "Neuroceoption, Interoception, and the Safety-Detection System," Mona Delahooke, *Brain-Body Parenting.* New York: HarperCollins, 2022, p.36. "Cues of safety," Deb Dana, *The Polyvagel Theory in Therapy: Engaging the Rhythm of Regulation.* New York: W. W. Norton, 2018, p.42.

6   Stuart Shanker, *Self-Reg: How to Help Your Child (and You) Break the Stress Cycle and Successfully Engage with Life.* New York: Penguin, 2016.

7   Stephen Porges, *The Pocket Guide to the Polyvagel Theory: The Transformative Power of Feeling Safe.* New York: W. W. Norton, 2017.

* * *

WHAT IS CO-REGULATION?

Stuart Shanker, in his book *Self-Reg*,[8] describes the "Still Face" experiment.[9] He tells the story of an infant lying in her mother's arms. As the two look at one another, the infant makes cooing faces, and the mother smiles back.

The mother then frowns and looks away, and the baby's physiological state responds. Her elevated heart rate, concerned facial expression, and whimpering all demonstrate her infant stress in the disconnection from her mother.

The mother looks back, smiles, reassuring her baby with her body signals that she is still safe, still connected.

In baby-mother brain scans, scientists have discovered that their brains are actually connecting on a subconscious level, as the baby draws on the parent to regulate.

Their brains signal stress, emotion, safety, connection, and love subconsciously, as both parent and child use their physiological brain-body connection to simultaneously move toward a state of steady calm.

Regulation is the ability to manage and control stress. When we are dysregulated, or unable to manage stressors, we also lose the ability to use self-control.[10] Therefore, on a brain level, kids who are stressed are not able to make the best choices.

When we disconnect from kids, this greatly exacerbates their stress, which then makes them more likely to act in ways that we would call "bad behavior." This behavior is actually a stress response, not a behavioral one. If their brains were calm and

---

8   Stuart Shanker, *Self-Reg: How to Help Your Child (and You) Break the Stress Cycle and Successfully Engage with Life*. New York: Penguin, 2016.
9   E.Z. Tronick, "Emotions and Emotional Connection in Infants," *American Psychologist 1989*, 44, 112–119.
10 Mona Delahooke calls this having an "unstable platform." Mona Delahooke, *Brain-Body Parenting: How to Stop Managing Behavior and Start Raising Joyful, Resilient Kids*. New York: HarperCollins, 2022

regulated, managing their stress well, they would show the positive behaviors that adults want to see.

In a cruel twist, when adults punish stress behaviors with disconnection, it ramps up children's stress, leading to more stress behaviors, and more punishment. It is a downward spiral of disconnection and pain.

On the other side, like the infant in the example above, when kids draw near to stable, emotionally attuned adults and actively mirror their emotional state, they manage their stress and return to a calm state. When the baby looked at her mother, she saw a brain in a state of calm connection, which she then mirrored back. In other words, children literally borrow an adult's brain, specifically the prefrontal cortex, the part of the brain responsible for regulation, control, and planning. If you've ever felt mentally exhausted being around your child, this may make you feel less crazy! In connected adult–child relationships, our brain is literally working overtime to help our child stay regulated, calm, and at ease.

* * *

WHAT THIS MEANS FOR PARENTING YOUR CHILD

You are not causing your child's difficult behavior by giving in to their demands. You are not making things worse by listening and empathizing when they kick, scream, hit, break things, and use awful words. No matter how drastic the behavior looks, it is still a stress response, a signal of a child who is suffering.[11]

We have reframed our children's meltdowns as panic attacks, which on a brain level, they are.[12]

The meltdown is a symptom of acute anxiety overload, a panicked brain caught in the survival pathway, unable to find a way to return to steady calm. No punishments, rewards, or self-control

---

11 Mona Delahooke, *Brain-Body Parenting: How to Stop Managing Behavior and Start Raising Joyful, Resilient Kids.* New York: HarperCollins, 2022.

12 Deb Dana, *The Polyvagal Theory in Therapy: Engaging the Rhythm of Regulation.* New York: W. W. Norton, 2018.

will improve this brain response, just as you cannot control the way your child's meltdowns cause your brain and body to react. The traditional parenting approach of punishments and rewards, combined with disconnection and disapproval, will deepen your child's stress and elevate their threat-response behavior. In other words, taking the traditional path will likely make things much worse.[13] It certainly did for us.

Seeing your child suffer is excruciating. You are allowed to be broken-hearted by your child's stress, even when they are screaming "I hate you" in your face. You are also allowed to be a human with a sensitive nervous system detecting threat. Meaning that if you feel like attacking back, running and hiding, or bending to their every whim to protect yourself, it's because you are a human under major stress. Your brain is in the fight-or-flight survival pathway, and you are trying to stay alive.[14]

We humans have a very difficult time feeling multiple conflicting things at once. But it is possible to feel broken-hearted for your child, scared for yourself, and angry for the threat to another child, all at once. What's important is how you respond to your suffering child.

Can you stay connected, even when the signs of their distress are distressing to you?

WHAT THIS MEANS FOR YOU

This is incredibly difficult work, but by adopting low-demand parenting, you will need to do it less and less. Low-demand parenting lessens everyone's stress, lowering the demand for you to co-regulate and manage your own stress. With fewer meltdowns, you can use your brain power for healing your own wounds and for showing

---

13 Ross Greene, *The Explosive Child: A New Approach for Understanding and Parenting Easily Frustrated, Chronically Inflexible Children.* New York: HarperCollins, 1998.
14 Mona Delahooke, *Brain-Body Parenting: How to Stop Managing Behavior and Start Raising Joyful, Resilient Kids.* New York: HarperCollins, 2022.

up to be present to your child in those (now rarer) moments of dysregulation.

Your brain will literally be better wired to handle these meltdowns, as you stay in your calm pathway, instead of going into the survival pathway.

This may seem impossible at first—and this may be a sign of trauma.

What you've lived through may be clinically severe, and you may need to get more support. I have had an intensive season of therapy to heal from my pain and parenting PTSD. I used trauma-informed yoga,[15] EMDR,[16] Somatic Experiencing,[17] Neurofeedback[18] and Polyvagel Listening therapy (like the Safe and Sound Protocol)[19] to heal.

You will likely need more support from a friend, partner, or trained professional as you undertake this parenting paradigm transformation.

I deeply encourage you to take a long look at your own stress levels and your brain-body responses. I could tell that my trauma was clinically severe because it was showing up in my relationship to my child, in my dreams, and in my body through stomach pain

---

15 For more on trauma-informed yoga, see scholarly research on effectiveness: Jennifer West, Belle Liang, and Joseph Spinazzola, "Trauma Sensitive Yoga as a complementary treatment for posttraumatic stress disorder: A Qualitative Descriptive analysis," *International Journal of Stress Management* 2017, 24(2): 173–195.

16 For more on Eye Movement Desensitization and Reprocessing (EMDR), see: emdr.com from the EMDR Institute, Inc., where peer reviewed and meta-analytic studies report steady and persistent benefit to EMDR, without requiring any additional homework for the patient during treatment.

17 For more on Somatic Experiencing, see the work of Peter Levine, *Healing Trauma: Restoring the Wisdom of the Body*, Aurorora: CA: SoundsTrue, 1999 and Peter Levine, *Healing Trauma: A Pioneering Program for Restoring the Wisdom of the Your Body*, Aurorora: CA: SoundsTrue, 2008. For seminal work on body-based treatments for healing trauma, see Bessel Van der Kolk, *The Body Keeps the Score: Brain, Mind and Body in the Healing of Trauma*. New York: Penguin Books, 2014.

18 Neurofeedback, also known as EEG Biofeedback, measures brain waves for a real-time, computer supported assessment of brainwave activity. Note: I used the NeurOptimal over the course of one month of treatment. mindbalance-neuro.com.

19 For more on the Safe and Sound Protocol by Stephen Porges, see integratedlistening.com. This listening protocol that draws on the polyvagel theory and work of Dr. Porges and must be administered by a trained therapist.

and digestive distress. I felt out of control, afraid, and alert for threat all the time.

It turns out that I needed to take steps toward managing my own sensitive threat response system in order to offer that calm steady brain to my children.

Chapter Three

Uniquely Wired Kids

NEURODIVERSITY

Neurodiversity is a movement to claim the many ways there are to be human.[1]

The neurodiversity movement says that uniquely wired human brains are a good and natural aspect of humanity's thriving diversity. Like the proliferation of diversity among plant and animal species, human diversity also exists for the wholeness of the species. We need unique brains to be a whole people.

Yet the neurodiversity movement also helpfully names the power of *ableism,* a corrosive power that elevates some brains and bodies over others, a power that says there is one best way to be human and that all other types are broken by comparison.[2]

Naming ableism means that we can say that *this world wasn't designed for the flourishing of all.*

It was designed for the flourishing of the few.

To be neurodiverse in an ableist world is to confront this power every day. It is social—meaning it is embedded in large social and societal dynamics, and it is personal—meaning it is embedded in my own heart and mind.

To remake the world for your child, you will confront ableism in yourself, in your partner, in your wider family, in your friendships, in the schooling system, in your community, and in the wider world.

---

1   To learn the history of this movement, see Steve Silberman, *Neurotribes: The Legacy of Autism and the Future of Neurodiversity.* New York: Avery, 2016.

2   Eric Garcia, *We're Not Broken: Changing the Autism Conversation.* Carlow, Ireland: Harvest Press, 2021.

This world wasn't made for all of us.

Uniquely wired children

In her seminal book *Differently Wired: Raising an Exceptional Child in a Conventional World*,[3] Deborah Reber, founder of Tilt Parenting, shares that one in five children are what she calls "differently wired." Reber's definition of differently wired includes a wide range of children, with a wide range of unique brains:

- ADHD

- learning differences (dyslexia, dysgraphia, dyscalculia)

- autism

- giftedness

- anxiety and OCD

- depression

- bipolar

- sensory processing disorder

- intellectual disabilities.

Other researchers who look at these overlapping and often co-occurring differences point to the core element of sensitivity that binds these different wirings together.[4]

Researchers can see this sensitivity on a brain level, as uniquely wired brains actually have novel neuronal connections.[5] Different brain connections lead to a different experience of the world. More

---

3 Deborah Weber, *Differently Wired: Raising an Exceptional Child in a Conventional World*. New York: Workman Publishing Group, 2018.

4 Jarena Nerenberg, *Divergent Mind: Thriving in a World that Wasn't Designed for You*. New York: HarperOne, 2021.

5 Guomei Tang, Kathryn Gudsnuk, Sheng-Han Kuo, Andrew J. Dwork, James Goldman, & David Sulzer, "Loss of mTOR-Dependent Macroautophagy Causes Autistic-like Synaptic Pruning Deficits." *Neuron* 2014, *83*(5), 1131–1143.

brain connections lead to a more intense experience of the world. A highly attuned body and brain can be a great gift, but in an overwhelming, fast-paced world, it is challenging for highly sensitive brains to get just what they need to remain regulated and ready to thrive.

These sensitive children may struggle with demands that others would not; they may need supports and accommodations that surprise and challenge the assumptions of the world. They may develop in asynchronous ways and require supports far longer than people say is "developmentally appropriate." The low-demand approach does not use any external measures to determine what demands are too hard for your unique child. Instead, this approach gets specific: this child in this moment, with this unique set of circumstances. There is no need to search Pinterest or chat rooms for fancy packages and materials to slap down on your life. You will work with your particular child and your own unique needs to develop a lifestyle and a relationship that honors your individual selves. This is a method to chart your own path.

Uniquely wired adults

As I found in my own investigations, neurodivergent children often come from families of neurodivergent adults. Parents, aunts, uncles, and grandparents are all increasingly likely to share neurodivergent traits with these uniquely wired kids. Despite helpful umbrellas like ADHD, autism, and giftedness, the reality is that every person's brain has extremely particular strengths, struggles and capacities. Low-demand parenting also accounts for the truth that you are also a unique individual, with your own traumas and life experiences, that will emerge and impact your parenting journey. You do not need to be an ideal version of yourself to follow this path. You do not need to leave your neurodivergence or childhood trauma at the door. Instead, you get to show up as you are, whether it's your best moment or your worst. You are who you are, and you will parent best from a place of authenticity and truth.

Low-demand for PDAers

Though the low-demand process works beautifully for a range of children, it is a necessity for many PDA children (and adults). PDA wires with an extreme and pervasive need for control and autonomy, which is in direct contrast to many popular parenting methods that emphasize children's deep-seated need for adults to remain in control at all times. These methods maintain a philosophical position that children only feel safe when they are with a confident caregiver who maintains healthy and firm boundaries. They declare that it is a child's job to test boundaries, but that children essentially need their adults to say, "No matter how you push, I will remain firm."

This approach can do massive damage to a PDA child. PDA children need the opposite truth: "No matter the situation, I can be free. Whatever I do, you will remain flexible." When a PDAer encounters a rigid adult boundary, they feel instinctively, subconsciously unsafe around this person. They feel as though they are being hunted by a wild animal, as though they are about to fall off a cliff to their own demise. Boundaries do not make them feel safe. The opposite is true. PDA children also suffer from the pervasive theory that they are "testing boundaries." These "testing" behaviors do not lessen as they encounter firm and confident adults—rather, they escalate and intensify. The resulting behaviors often get loud, aggressive, and violent, which leads to stigma and shame from adults. "What are you thinking? Why would you do that?" Adults glare and send them away, punishing the behavior without asking the real question: "What are you telling me here?" In truth, these actions are often arising out of their primary language for communicating with their caregivers—their bodies. They are autistic after all. They struggle with neurotypical norms of back-and-forth verbal conversation. Their primary mode of expression is through their bodies. They are attempting to say, "This is too hard for me, too much for me." Instead, their behavior is interpreted through a lens that says, "Naughty, bad, wrong."

An approach for PDA safety and thriving

PDAers thrive in a world where they have control and autonomy, the ability to captain their own ship. Even as young children, they see relationships through a lens of equity. They view all people as equally deserving of respect. They can be remarkable champions of children's liberation—the movement to give children freedom to pursue their own paths, instead of being controlled by adults. They dismantle the view that adults always know best, or what is becoming called "adultism." In contrast, they are advocates for a culture of consent and a radically inclusive family culture that respects every member equally, regardless of age.

To set a PDAer free to thrive, they must exist in safety and trust. Because their behavioral expressions are autonomic, on a subconscious brain level, they are not "trying" to be bad or aggressive. They are not communicating: "I need better boundaries. I need better self-control. I need to learn respect," as is commonly attributed to them. They are communicating: "I need freedom. I need control. I need autonomy in my own life." The way to freedom and control is a low-demand life. Dropping demands systematically is the primary support structure for reducing harmful behaviors and seeing your PDAer shine.

BEYOND DIAGNOSIS

Having or knowing specific diagnoses is not necessary for the purposes of this approach. Low-demand parenting also works well with neurotypical kids, and for those who have a mixed neurology family, you can (and I recommend you do) use the same approach with all your children. All children have difficulties and express it in their own ways. A diagnosis may simply be a list or blanket term for the behaviors your child uses to express their difficulty.

Difference is difference—and if you have a sense you are raising a uniquely wired child, you are! Your intuition is trustworthy. If you don't have a name or diagnosis yet for your child's unique brain, you can breathe. You belong here, and this method will give you a path to follow to develop your own parenting approach custom-made for you, your family, and your unique child.

For the purpose of this low-demand method, we will lean less on a diagnosis and more on the specifics of your family and your child. This can be freeing for some, and scary for others. For now, we will treat a diagnosis or label as a helpful guide pointing to places of passion, strength, uniqueness, and difficulty.

If your child has a brain-body disability, meaning a distinct bio-neurological makeup, we will treat this with the same reverence as we would if they had a physical disability. If your child had a physical difference that prevented them from doing certain things, would you continue to expect them to be able to do them? If your child was born without typically developing legs, would you expect them to walk up the stairs on the same timetable as other children? When the difference exists in their brain makeup, it is no less disabling.

Chapter Four

What Are Demands?

Demands have many layers, both for the child and the adult. Demands are essentially solutions to problems, so letting go of demands can feel like dropping all the tools in your toolbox or unleashing all your problems with no solution in sight. In other words, it can be really scary.

Demand

Expectation

Need

There's the demand itself on the surface, then underneath the demand is the expectation, or the positive thing that you hope the child will do, and then under that is the adult's need, hope, or desire.

For example:

The *demand* is to stop hitting your brother right now.

The *expectation* is that you will learn to be gentle with others.

The *adult need* is a little silence because I'm overstimulated after a long and noisy day and when you hit, your little brother screams, and it is too loud for my poor ears.

We are demand-factories.

We do not know how many demands we are churning out all the time. Expectations are how we structure our days. You likely have a picture of the flow of your day in your head, even if it doesn't have any obvious structure to an outside observer.

We like for things happen in certain ways because it enables our brains to rest. We may sit in the same chair at the dinner table or squeeze our toothpaste from the same side of the tube. We may take our medicine at a specific time or in a specific way.

You likely also have a picture of how your child moves through their day, even if it appears chaotic.

To begin to see with the eyes of a low-demand parent, you must begin to view the world with an eye for threat, because demands can feel like threats to your child. To drop them, you need to see them. To see them, you need to look at everyday events with new eyes.

To look at the demands you have to stop looking at the behaviors.

All the crying, refusing, hitting, kicking, screaming, breaking, melting down and flipping out. All the cursing and yelling and slamming doors. All the ways that your life feels unsustainably hard. You are going to shift your sights, and this is hard. Things feel terrible *right now,* and you want a solution that will work quickly. This will work, and it will likely work quickly, but it takes a good bit of parent effort. It may require a conscious setting aside of your reward charts, your ABC (antecedent, behavior, consequence) methodologies, and going against what other experts and books are telling you to do.

There are other experts at the top of their respective fields who support this approach—including brain scientists, psychologists, and speech, occupational and behavioral therapists (check out the Further Reading section at the end of the book to find these experts).

I am giving you permission to *stop listening to people who tell you that your child is wilful, disobedient, and is testing you,* and that the answer is to be firmer, to have better routines and better boundaries. This is not your fault. You are not going to "discipline" your way out of an unsustainably hard place.

You are also not alone drowning at the bottom of a well with no bucket.

Yes, you and your child are off the standard path. You may feel like you are wandering in the deep dark woods with no map. This book is your map and your flashlight. It will not tell you what you will see or what to do. But it will show you how to keep walking and will shine a light on what's really going on. With these tools, you get to find your own way—a beautiful, rich, trusting, connected, and engaged life with your unique child that can work for you both. You can build a relationship that will guide you through all your days.

But first, you have to stop looking at behavior and start looking at demands.

✳ ✳ ✳

"CAN'T," NOT "WON'T"

As you shift your sights away from your child's behavior, this is a moment to also shift your interpretation of the meaning of their behavior. To replace your old vision with a new, fresh one. Since our children are hard-wired for connection and are intrinsically motivated to do their best to please us, when they are not able to meet our expectations (think: behavior), it's because they can't do it, not that they won't do it.[1] They are not doing it to challenge you, control you, punish you, or test your boundaries. Something is getting in their way. If they could do it, they would. It's a "can't do it", not a "won't do it."

When your child refuses to do something or melts down in the process or gets so distracted they don't complete the task, it's because they can't. There is something amiss, yes, but it is not motivation. They may have a uniquely wired brain. They may lack skills. Anxiety may be crippling. Depression may sap the energy needed. Slow processing speed may be hindering their ability to make sense of the request. Executive functioning may not be in place to attend to the steps involved. Attention differences may distract at the crucial moment.

For many of our uniquely wired kids, anxiety and brain differences are a dominant feature of their lives. Imagine that your child is a wild gazelle, grazing in an open plain. Suddenly they hear the

---

1   Ross Greene, *The Explosive Child: A New Approach for Understanding and Parenting Easily Frustrated, Chronically Inflexible Children.* New York: Harper, 2014.

snap of a twig that may be a lion, lying in wait to attack.[2] That simple "snap" has them frozen. Every biological process has altered because of this one single sound, all to protect them from imminent death. If you walked up to the gazelle, not having heard that "snap" and demanded that they go on eating grass, they would not be able to do it. Their brain was not evolved to move from imminent death to happy grazing in a flash.

A biological process has begun that has a beginning, middle, and an end. It must complete in order for the gazelle to leave this survival mode and return to grazing.

Many of our uniquely wired kids are like that gazelle who has been hunted all their lives. They are equipped with a brain that hears every twig snapping and that flips into survival mode on a dime. Those of us who are not wired that way, or who are but did not experience the same trigger, cannot simply ask them to go back to their happy grazing.

The next time your child flips into survival mode (you know what this looks like for your kid, I don't need to list the behaviors), say to yourself, "It's a *can't*, not a *won't*."

But you are not stuck here. Instead, you get to transform everything without making your child be someone they are not. You can accept this uniquely wired brain and the lack of skills. You can start right where you are without shame, blame, or judgment. You just need to start looking at demands.

FINDING THE BIG DEMANDS

Demands exist throughout the day. There are big, anchoring demands around events like mealtimes, hygiene, and school. There are tiny, itty-bitty demands like putting up your hand for a high-five and expecting your child to high-five you back.

---

2   Peter Levine walks his listeners through such a "prey" experience in his book *Healing Trauma* (Louisville, CO: Sounds True, 2008) as he offers Somatic Experiencing techniques for restoration after experiences of trauma.

To begin to identify the demands of your child's day, fill in the Day-Flow Worksheet in the Resources section with a demand lens. What big demands structure your child's waking, eating, playing/learning, and bedtime routines? By "big demands," I mean the things that are easily visible.

As we will explore, there are many subtle demands that are harder to see and name, but just as powerful, especially as you try to take steps forward with this approach.

waking

get out of bed and walk downstairs, brush teeth

breakfast eating

sit at the table, choose what to eat, be kind to parents and siblings, put your plate away

playing/learning

learn, listen to teachers or parents, follow directions, engage with siblings or students

eating

eat at set times, eat nourishing parent-approved food, eat around others

playing/learning

remember and respect screen-time limits, share with siblings, tolerate disruption

eating

talk about your day, listen as adults talk, sit still, use knife and fork, eat what is served

bedtime

brush teeth, change clothes, choose pyjamas, go to sleep on time

These big demands are often the places where we see big behavior from our kids. We may see full resistance to parts of this day-flow.

You may see patterns already in the demands that are hardest for your child to manage. However, it is also important to begin to see the tiny demands that may be just as challenging for your child.

FINDING THE TINY DEMANDS

Here are some questions to begin to brainstorm all the many, many demands that may be baked into a situation:

1. What must be stopped to meet the expectation?
2. How must it be stopped to meet the expectation?
3. When does this expectation need to happen?
4. How quickly must it happen?
5. By a certain time?
6. Will it be a race, and does the child need to be first?
7. What must happen before or after?
8. Where must it happen?
9. In a certain position?
10. With specific items?
11. What order must it be done in?
12. Must it be done quietly?
13. Who else is there at the same time?
14. Alone or with help?
15. Which helper?
16. With spoken words?
17. With specific spoken words?

18. With listening to spoken words?

19. With listening to specific spoken words?

20. What happens once the expectation is done?

Practical demand example: Putting on shoes

What must be stopped to meet the expectation?

Is the child sitting on the couch watching TV, half-way through a Lego set, or finishing a snack right next to the shoe bucket? These situations are each completely different and will invoke different demands depending on what needs to stop in order to move to the shoe demand.

How must it be stopped to meet the expectation?

Does the child need to stop watching tv by pausing their show, switching it over onto their tablet? Does the Lego need to be put away or can it be contained to keep it safe from a little sibling?

When?

Does the child need to start putting on their shoes right now? Do the shoes need to go on at a specific time (e.g., in five minutes) or can it happen following the child's own internal clock (when I'm done with this Lego set)? Is the adult in charge of the "When" or is the child?

How quickly?

Do the shoes need to go on quickly, or can they go be done at the kid's own pace? Will there be prompts to hurry or to keep moving? If the kid does it super-fast, will they then have to wait, and what would this waiting be like?

By what time?

Is there some external timer ticking like a soccer practice or a grandparent waiting in the car?

Will it be a race? Does the child need to be the first one to do it?

Does the child have their own internal demand to be first at putting on their shoes today? Will it feel like a race to anyone involved?

What must happen before or after?

Does the child have to move to a different location to put their shoes on? Do old socks have to come off for fresh ones to go on? Do they also have to put on a coat or gloves or hat once shoes are on? Are these demands linked in the child's mind?

Where must it happen?

Do you put on shoes in a noisy chaotic hallway? Will there be people touching your child there? Does the carpet have a texture that must be tolerated? Can the shoes come to the child right where they are?

What position must it happen in?

Can they lay down prone and have you put the shoes on? Can they hang upside down on the sofa and put on their own shoes? Is there a demand that it be done sitting in a certain way?

What item(s) must the child use?

Do they get to pick their socks and shoes? Is there a demand that they pick out shoes and socks themselves, or a demand that they accept what you pick? Can they make a weather-inappropriate choice like sandals on a cold day or winter boots in summer?

What order must it be done in?

Shoes and socks have to happen in one order—socks first and then shoes. Other demands may have more flexibility in the order of things. Can it happen backwards? Can novelty be introduced into the order of the demands somehow? Could the child put on a coat first, and then socks and shoes? Could the child go outside, then put on their shoes on the porch?

Must it be done quietly?

Is there an expectation that things happen at a certain volume? Is there a demand for no whining or complaining?

Who else is there at the same time?

Who is around while shoes go on? Is someone watching or can the child do it alone, without eyes?

Alone or with help?

Does the child require help with getting their foot into the shoe or with tying laces? Do they have to ask with words, or can there be a hand signal? Is the mere fact of requiring help a demand?

Which helper?

Does it have to be mom or dad or a sibling? Can the child choose who helps?

With spoken words?

Are spoken words required in this interaction? Are there nonverbal ways that communication could happen?

With specific spoken words?

Are *please* and *thank you* and *I'm sorry* required words? Are there other mandated words specific to this situation?

With listening to spoken words?

Does this demand require that the child hear certain words? Are you talking on the phone or to a partner or to a child while the child is putting on their shoes?

With listening to specific spoken words?

Can the child have control over what you say as well as what they say? Perhaps you always give a time count as people are getting shoes on, such as "Two more minutes!" Could the child choose for you not to say it or to say it in a silly voice?

What happens once the expectation is done?

Once the shoes are on, is it to go to a fun event like the park, or to a dentist appointment? The purpose of putting on the shoes will very much impact the demand of putting them on.

Low-demand parenting will take into account all of these demands, and obviously there are a *lot*, just in the one simple demand of "put on your shoes." Low-demand parents will begin to drop even the small subtle demands, like things happening in a certain place or a certain order.

It's true that some demands cannot be dropped. Many can.

You may already be dropping demands out of necessity. Your child simply will not get up from the couch to walk to the shoe bin, so you begin bringing them to your child on the couch. They will not put them on themselves, so you begin to put them on, even though your kid is "old enough" to do it themselves, or a younger sibling can do it already.

Many of these out-of-necessity dropped demands are frustrating and demoralizing to parents. They steal our joy and sap our energy. We will call this dropping a demand in the moment.

HOW TO DROP A DEMAND IN THE MOMENT

- You ask them to do something, and they scream "No!" You then say, "Ok."

- If they start having visible difficulty, stop doing what you are doing immediately. See if it helps.

- When you suggest something that they do not want to do, say "Oops. Never mind. You don't have to."

- Do it for them, instead of asking them to do it independently.

- Do it with them, instead of asking them to do it alone.

- Let them go home early from an event.

- Let them watch a show on your phone or play a video game in the moment if you can't make the full demand go away (e.g., stuck at soccer practice and can't make sibling leave practice early).

- Let them play by themselves or read in a corner, ignoring other people's desires for them to interact.

- Say "You can have it" when they want something you don't want them to have (e.g., kid sees ice cream in the freezer and asks to eat it, you say "yes").

- Buy the thing they have decided they need, even though it's not a good day to do it or you don't think they need it.

You're only going to get so far by dropping demands in the moment like this.

That said, it's better to drop a demand in the moment than to hold onto the demand in the moment.

But *in the moment* will not work well for you, and it won't work well for your child. You will not see the full healing that you are looking for. The need to drop a demand in the moment is a signal to you that you've got more work to do proactively. Write down the situation and work it through using the system below. You can always defuse your grenade. But even better if you never pull the pin in the first place.

BE AWARE OF THE FAKE DROP

When I first started with low-demand parenting, I thought it meant that I had to drop all expectations, everywhere and in every way, and I tried that, but my chest felt tight and I felt burdened. I realized that my chest was tight from holding back all the time. I was holding my expectations back from my kids, but that left me burdened and exhausted because my needs and desires just kept piling in my arms. This led to *fake-dropping demands*, building desperation and resentment in me, and meant I was not getting my real needs met.

Remember:

DEMAND

EXPECTATION

NEED

Demands sit on top of expectations of behavior you'd like to see, and on top of an adult need. Fake-dropping demands is when you drop the immediate demand but do not process the expectation or adult need beneath it. You drop the demand but not the underlying belief that it matters and that your child should be doing it.

You fake-drop brushing teeth by bringing it up each night and then sighing when they throw a fit. You fake-drop food rules by continuing to serve the foods you want them to eat first, and only getting up to make an alternate meal when they refuse to eat what you served.

A painful fake-drop for me was for my son who does not like to be touched. Being touched unexpectedly is a demand that he cannot handle. It sends his autonomic nervous system into fight or flight and feels like an existential threat. But I really like to hug him. So, I fake-dropped the demand that he hug me goodnight. I no longer asked him to do it, but I wished he would. I wished he would be the kind of kid who hugs his mom. I felt sad and wistful every night, saying goodnight without touching him at all. I played this scenario out into the future, worrying that he would not be able to embrace a partner or a friend, that he would be lonely and singular and strange.

This was a fake-drop because I did not deal with the real reasons that hugging is important to me, and because I did not identify the deep reason that I was dropping this expectation.

Like the "in the moment" drop, a "fake-drop" is also better than nothing. But it will not get you where you want to go and can quickly lead to burnout. Fake-dropping demands is where most of us get stuck and can make parents bitter about the concept of low-demand parenting.

If it's only low-demand for the child, but very high demand for the adults, then is it really better?

This is an important and valid question. For the lifestyle to be truly freeing and truly life-giving, it also needs to release the adults from the demand-factory of modern life.

Moreover, our highly sensitive kids can feel the difference between a true release of expectations and a fake-drop. They will know that we continue to be disappointed and unhappy, that we still think they should be able to do this thing. This will lead to shame and disconnection. It will sabotage our relationship, right when we are trying so hard to make a radical move toward connection.

Your frustration and resentment are the key factors to observe.

Frustration and resentment are indicators that you've done a fake drop, and that you have unmet needs. You've successfully dropped a demand, but you have not processed the expectation and found the true "why" beneath it. We always start with our own true needs because once we meet our own needs, we are free to shut down the demand factory and begin exploring the new relationships that open up with our loved ones.

Chapter Five

How to Drop Demands

HOW TO ACTUALLY DROP A DEMAND

There are six steps to effectively drop a demand:

1. Put words to the demand itself.

2. Find out why this matters to you.

3. Listen to your child.

4. Work proactively to drop demands.

5. Get creative in taking care of your own needs—without asking your child to do anything differently.

6. Create house rules.

1. Put words to the demand itself

This might be a good time to take a look at the Day-Flow Worksheet you've already filled out from the Resources section, or if you haven't gotten to it yet, perhaps you want to take a break and begin to fill it in. What is the flow of your day, and what big demands can you identify? Then try to choose one and use the questions above to determine what demands could be dropped, fully and wholeheartedly.

You may want to print the explicit demand at the top of your page if you are using a journal to work through this process, or use the guide in the Resources section. Be as specific as possible. If you just write "putting on shoes," you will not get where you want to go. Each situation is different, and solvable, and the more specific you are, the easier it gets.

As you get started, choose a very small, very specific demand to drop. Let go of the demand that your child wear matching socks. Or if your child always needs to be the first to get their socks and shoes on, let them be first every time. The size of the demand isn't what matters. The process you go through to drop the demand is what matters. So, take your time here, and define the demand really specifically.

Breakfast meltdowns

For example, when we got started, I desperately wanted to solve the kitchen meltdowns in the morning. These meltdowns disrupted everyone as we started our day. It was hard on my nervous system to be yelled at before I'd had any coffee. I also knew that getting food into my son was essential to his regulation. I was really focused on the behaviors, throwing food, screaming, hitting his siblings, difficulty choosing what he wanted, changing his mind, and being incredibly picky with the bowl, spoon, and milk provided.

But I had to look *earlier*, before the meltdowns, to the demands and expectations that came first. I couldn't drop demands until I knew what they were. So I wrote, "eat breakfast" as my demand (knowing that there were many more demands embedded), and then I went through the 20 questions in the previous chapter to find the layers of demands.

I discovered the place (a noisy kitchen with every member of our family), the method (verbal conversation with a grouchy un-caffeinated grown-up), and the act itself (pouring out the cereal, waiting for milk, eating the cereal) were all demands. They all went onto my piece of paper, and I moved on to step 2.

* * *

2. Find out why this matters to you

(You get to hold onto that "why", even though you are also dropping a demand)

Your "why" is the *most* important part of this process, and it may take time to get to the true why, particularly as you get started.

It may feel like the why is simply a set of parent rules:

Good parents do _____.

Good parents feed their kids healthy food.

Good parents make sure their kids wear shoes outside.

Good parents have kids who turn in their homework.

Good parents teach their kids respect.

Sadly, these parenting rules are not serving you anymore (and did they ever?), so it's time to set them aside and dig deeper. Some parents do not have to question these rules or wonder why they exist. You are not one of those parents.

I'll skip right to the good stuff:

Our big goal here is to *take care of your why* without asking your kid to do anything differently.

Achieve your bigger goal while dropping your demand! Beautiful right?!

Is this impossible? No.

Is it challenging? At first. (Ok, *I'll be honest*, it's always challenging but it does get easier.)

Is it worth it? Hells to the yes!

The big news here is that this process of digging into your "why" will transform your life.

By finding out why you are holding onto certain expectations with your kids, you will also discover why you tick and how you operate and bring those processes into your conscious awareness. No auto-pilot parenting for you.

If you have inherited parenting practices from prior generations that caused you pain as a child, this will be a process of deprogramming and interrupting generational trauma so that you do not pass this painful childhood experience onto your child.

I highly recommend that you bring these revelations to a trained professional counselor who can guide you through the deep work of inner healing at the same time as you parent your real-life child.

If you want to know more and know that you will not be able to find a therapist anytime soon, here's a quick way to try it: Picture you as a child. Hold a picture of Little You, and actually shape your arms as though you are giving this Little You a hug.

Give this kiddo some straight up mental loving.

Say, "You really had it hard. I know. Tell me more," and then sit with this little part of you and listen. You may hear a lot of stuff. With all you hear, send back love.

If it helps, pretend this is your child, crying and struggling, and send endless empathy and compassion. The more you love and have compassion for the child you used to be, the more you will be able to love and have compassion on your own flesh and blood child. (But I want to add one more appeal for a trained professional counselor because you deserve that sort of focused attention on this inner work.)

Discerning your "why": What do I hope they will learn by letting this go?

One way to identify what really matters to you is to imagine what you hope your child will learn from this dropped expectation.

Let's take the example of my child who doesn't like to be touched.

I hope my child will learn to honor his unique bodily needs and always advocate for his own bodily boundaries.

I never want anyone to touch him in ways that make him anxious.

I want for all the people who love him to also love his body differences, to truly treasure his uniqueness, not merely to tolerate it.

I want to be a source of safety and regulation.

I want for my presence to calm him, not to send him into an unconscious anxiety response.

Now when I get up from his bed without a hug, I do so confident that this is the right choice. I imagine him whole, calm, settled and able to sleep without anxiety, and it is an honor to give him this gift.

Discerning your "why": Ask why, why, why, why, why?

You will need to dig deeply to discover why these demands and expectations matter to you. The first reason will not be the deep reason. So you start with "why?", and then ask why does that matter? And why does that matter? And why does that matter? Just keep asking until you feel a twinge in the pit of your stomach. The real stuff will likely create a bodily reaction. Those are the deep reasons, the things we must look at if we are truly going to change our lives.

Keep going until you get to the core of it. If you find you are having trouble dropping a demand, you may want to return to this process.

You may not have gotten deep enough to find the true core.

Resentment is your signal that you didn't get to the core of your "why." You probably have needs and priorities that are being missed.

For example, I wanted my son to put two bottom cheeks on his chair at mealtimes, and it annoyed me no end when he would stand next to the chair with one leg tucked up on the chair and one leg on the ground. I expected him to sit flat every meal, and every meal I was frustrated.

Why does my son's bottom being flat on his chair matter to me?

Because I want him to sit still at the table and not get up and down all the time.

Why do I want him to sit still and not get up?

Because it's distracting to everyone when he leaves the table and makes it harder for his brothers to eat their food.

Why do I want his brothers to eat their food?

Because they are already so hard to feed and never really want what I make.

Why do I want them to eat what I make?

Because one kid has such a limited diet and I'm worried that he isn't eating enough food.

Why do I want him to eat enough food?

So he will be able to survive and grow.

What really mattered to me at the table wasn't the number of cheeks on a chair or even my wiggly son at all. I was really worried about a different child all together. And by focusing on my concern that he survive and grow, I was able to see that he is doing both of those things.

Yes, he has a very limited diet, but we are actually able to expand this diet and focus on getting him new foods by taking a new approach to food anyway. I did not need to insist on everyone sitting at the table to solve the problem of survival and growth.

I can solve that 100 other ways that allow a wiggly kid to wiggle.

(And it turned out that the wiggly child wasn't uncomfortable at the table for no reason. We discovered that he has *misophonia,* a hypersensitive auditory condition that made it torturous for him to listen to us chewing. He wiggled and ran from the table out of pure survival energy. When we allowed him to eat privately, he was incredibly relieved and happy. Yield: A dropped demand, a delighted kid, a happy household, and a proud mother.)

Discerning your "why": What is it about really?

Another formula for landing on the true reasons that something is important is to ask a question:

What is it about (expectation/demand) that (positive result you want to happen)?

Some examples:

My son's breakfast struggles: I wanted my son to sit and eat his cereal so I could drink coffee in peace.

What is it about drinking coffee that brings me peace?

Daily frustration that my kids wouldn't take a walk with me in the afternoons.

What is it about long walks that helps in the afternoon?

Once I had worked out what really mattered by digging deeper into why that solution has worked for me in the past (or worked for me in my mental fantasies), I was in a position to decide whether to prioritize meeting my need in that way, or find an alternative solution.

For me, I am an empath, so others' emotions fill me to overflowing and confuse me simultaneously. The coffee not only got my brain going with caffeine, but a peaceful moment in the morning made me feel like myself and gave me time to wake up my emotions slowly. Now that I know why that morning cup of coffee matters to me, I can prioritize it, while dropping other demands related to my child's breakfast experience. By finding a calm breakfast routine that actually works for my child, I am also filling my cup (with coffee).

Afternoon walks worked for me because I experience a depressive lull in the afternoons. I am a morning person, and by 3pm, my energy is seriously flagging. Walking is a solution to rev up my brain with exercise and fresh air so I can make it through to bedtime without the feeling of burnout. Now that I know what need this solution meets, I can brainstorm other ways to get fresh air or afternoon exercise that don't ask my child to do anything differently.

3. Listen to your child

This can be the fun part, the scary part, the strangest part. But this is the part where you hear from your child about their experience.

Low-demand parenting happens in communication with your child. Low-demand parenting is pure guesswork without listening closely to your child.

Listening doesn't need to involve any words.

My son Michael loves to communicate with me as a puppy. Puppy can say he is hungry, needs to go to the bathroom, and needs water without any words. Puppy nuzzles me with his nose when he wants to snuggle, and climbs into my lap, wiggling, when he wants his back rubbed.

Your child's primary method of communication may be body-based. They may groan, roar, grunt, cry, run, thrash, wiggle, bite, kick, scream, throw, punch. They may also rub, snuggle, hang on you, and pull your hands. They are communicating with you in such meaningful ways, and you get to be a detective and an anthropologist to listen to this child's native tongue as they tell you about their experience.

For a season, you may want to pretend that your child doesn't use mouth words at all (and if they truly don't use mouth words, no problem, you're right at home here!). Or if your child is not currently communicating with you in any way (not speaking to you, or in a season of burnout), you can absolutely use this method. These behaviors and actions are still meaningful communication.

If your child couldn't or didn't speak, how would you know that things were or were not working? I use a category I call "meaningful communication."

- Screaming "go away" is meaningful communication that the child needs space.

- Pulling me by the hand away from the soccer field toward the car is meaningful communication that the child is ready to go home.

- Turning the iPad back on during a conversation is meaningful communication that they are done talking.

This helps separate me from my own demand-factory that my child communicate with me in calm, medium-volume, kind words (the typical adult-preferred method of communication) and accept the meaningful communication my child is offering.

If I want to know their experience, it is my job to listen as they share it in their own way.

To listen to your child, you need to create an environment where they are able to share. When my child was in burnout, he stopped communicating with me in words, and the energy he sent my way was all anger and frustration. He meaningfully communicated that he did not want to see me ("Get out of my face!"). He meaningfully communicated that he needed space from all sights and sounds (closed and locked door). He meaningfully communicated that he was upset when his boundaries were crossed (growling when someone entered his space).

I listened deeply to his emotions and his boundaries and decided that my deep why for this season was healing and trust. I wanted to trust him that he knew his body and knew his needs. That this too could be trusted.

I wanted to proactively drop every single possible demand so that I could communicate to my son that I saw he was at capacity and that I respected this season in his life. So, I no longer knocked on the door and asked if he wanted water, I just quietly set a full water cup down outside his door, slid a picture of a cup under the door to let him know it was there, and took the empty one away later. When he left the door open or I brought him snacks, I didn't make eye contact or touch him; I just left what he needed and walked out.

My energy said, "I see and respect your boundaries. I love you here and will still take care of you when you are furious with me." This aligned with my deep why—trust that he would connect with me in his own way, when he was ready, and a focus on healing our relationship with understanding and compassion.

Our children sense our energy deeply and are always scanning to see if they are safe. As their parent or caregiver, it is important to recognize that your child is reading your nonverbal and energetic signals more than your explicit verbal ones. If you say, "I see that you're angry with me" to affirm them, but your energy says, "I'm pissed that you're angry with me," it will likely deepen the gap between you.

You communicate respect and avoid triggering your child's threat system by slowing down your words, calming your tone (think a meditation app voice), smiling with your eyes and mouth, relaxing your shoulders and hands, and squatting down low to the ground. I have a mantra of "gentle and genuine" for my curiosity. I really genuinely want to know, but I am gentle in my pursuit and willing to stop at any point.

Your heart posture and energy matter most.

That said, sometimes you do get to use words.

Verbal conversations typically involve a question and an answer, but here's the deal:

Questions are not likely to work well for your child.

Questions are a very intense demand for many children. If your child loves to answer questions, then you are in luck and can move ahead with question-and-answer style conversation. But if not, you may need to try a new style of conversation that opens up room for, but does not demand, a response.

It's also possible that maybe you've never really listened to your child talk about their experience of their own difficulty. If so, they are probably used to talking about the behaviors themselves (e.g., Why did you kick your brother? Why are you screaming at me?), while absorbing your disappointed and frustrated energy.

They may be really hesitant to talk to you, and you may want to throw this whole method in the trash because your child won't participate. That's ok. You do *not* need your child to do anything differently in order to move forward. They do not need to talk to you. That's a demand. You can let that go too.

Use declarative language instead

As you consider a conversation with your child, practice your declarative language. Declarative language is a statement or an observation that does not ask anything specific of the listener.[1]

Declarative language will observe something about a situation, narrate something happening, or notice a fact your child may have missed. Declarative language contrasts with imperative language—a question or a sentence that demands a response, whether a verbal response or an action (e.g. "It's time to stop your video" versus "I wonder how much time is left in your video").

Declarative sentences you might try:

I wonder if...

I'm curious about...

I have a guess that...

---

1 Linda Murphy, *Declarative Language Handbook: Using a Thoughtful Language Style to Help Kids with Social Learning Challenges Feel Competent, Connected, and Understood.* Linda Murphy, 2020.

I'm not sure if I am getting this right...

I'm thinking that...

For me, I notice... (state something true about yourself that may or may not be true for them).

Here's an example of how a conversation might work using declarative language:

I like to start a conversation at a calm and open moment by saying simply: "I was wondering if you could help me with something." (Your child may enjoy being the helper, the one solving the problem.)

My kid is usually cautiously curious: "Ok," or "With what?"

This is where you want to take a conscious step away from behaviors, away from demands, and toward your underlying "why it matters": "About leaving for soccer practice without stress."

Kid, open to the conversation, might say words or might not. ("Ok." "Yeah.") Or simply not ending the conversation may be a sign you can go forward. You may check in, "I'm feeling curious about your thoughts." I would put up my thumb as I say that, a nonverbal cue that I wonder if it's ok to continue or not. My kid can give a thumbs up back, or push my thumb down to show that he's not ok.

You can borrow this nonverbal communication or work on one of your own. How does your child currently signal agreement or disagreement nonverbally?

You can also use the low-demand communication tool in the Resources section, laying it beside you as you begin the conversation and pointing to images to support your words.

Now, assuming you're getting affirmation to move forward, you name a demand that is hard for them, acknowledging that you've already done your homework and noticed that it's really too hard: "I'm not sure if I'm getting this right, but I guess that something about putting on shoes is too hard when we're heading to soccer."

Depending on your kid, you may:

- receive a confident, "Oh, no, shoes aren't hard." In which case your guess that it was the shoes didn't pan out. You might try another guess, or state, "Oh ok, so it's not the shoes. I wonder if there's something else that's hard about getting to soccer practice without stress." (Maybe it's the socks, the shin guards, something about practice, you'll have to find out...)

- get a massive stream of words about what's too hard about shoes, and then they will want to end the conversation immediately

- hear silence as they are thinking. It's ok to let silence linger. Slow processing speed is real, and it means that the system is still working. Don't introduce any more words that need to be processed

- see a blank stare or "I don't know!" signaling that they've gone blank or genuinely don't know or cannot put words to what might be hard about it. You may move into some cueing. Pick just a few educated guesses. Stop guessing *as soon as* you see any indication of stress. This is important. If they are already stressed, you can simply stop here, affirm them for being open to the conversation, and indicate that you can talk about it later.

"I wonder if it's extra hard when your brother is around."

(This time you may visually offer your thumbs up, a thumbs sideways, or thumbs down as possible responses.)

"I wonder if it's hard when I need to tie the shoes."

"I wonder if it's hard to stop playing your Playstation to put on shoes."

"I wonder if you're worried about practice."

Remember, you are a demand detective.

Your whole goal here is to suss out any further demands that you may not have seen, so you can get creative with them or straight up drop them.

Focus on their thoughts, not their feelings

If feelings come, that's great. Validate them. But for many of our kids, thoughts are easier to access and are more helpful for your process. You likely see their feelings expressed nonverbally (sadness, anger, frustration, stress, anxiety, disappointment, fear). You likely know these feelings well. The question is what thoughts go along with them in these challenging situations that will help you drop further demands that may be triggering these big emotions.

Seek meaningful communication

Note meaningful communication of any type, even if it is recognizing that they said "Shut up!" immediately after you asked about racing a sibling. A clue perhaps?

I recommend taking notes after these conversations with your child, jotting down any observations, words, phrases, or themes that emerge. For one thing, you may forget what your child said. And for another, it's hard to notice change and transformation, and you may find that over time, your child's trust in you grows. You may find that they talk more, open up to you more, and use more words with you. You may not find that to be true, and it's all ok. It is about trust, and your child's trust may show up in other, non-conversation driven ways.

4. Work proactively to solve problems creatively

Now you have completed the "information gathering" part of your mission. You have a list of demands, including the tiny ones. You have dug deeply into your "why," and discerned what adult need underpins these expectations. You have listened to your child's meaningful communication, including all their nonverbal communication, to make an even longer, fuller list of demands. What next?

I recently traveled alone after years of not getting on an airplane nor going anywhere beyond our town. I was incredibly excited and incredibly anxious. I had an early flight, so I did everything I possibly could days in advance.

I made a list of all the things I needed to bring with me and did a big load of laundry so I could pack just what I wanted to wear. I set the coffee pot the night before and tucked my phone charger into my backpack.

I was working proactively to limit the demands on me in the morning, so that I could focus on what really mattered—staying calm and saying goodbye to my kids, who are early risers and were eager to see me off.

You get to work proactively too. Instead of managing explosions and meltdowns in the moment, you can now begin to align with your deeper "why" and drop demands for everyone proactively. Notice I said *for everyone*—you get to lessen the demands on you too.

Return to the lists you made in step 1 and work through the lists of demands embedded in your chosen scenario. Make it a game with yourself. How many can you drop proactively and definitively? (Keep your eyes peeled for frustration or resentment, a sign you've got to return to the "why" step).

With your "demand detective" hat on, can you look at that invitation from a neighbor to meet at the park with a new lens? What demands can you drop proactively?

Perhaps you tell them ahead of time that you may only be able to stay 15 minutes and use some of the scripts in the Resources section to reduce the demand that you explain an early exit in the moment.

Maybe you bring an iPad with proactively downloaded videos to lessen the demand that you cut a good conversation with your friend short when your child decides they're done playing at the park.

Perhaps you choose a play idea ahead of time (like soccer or stuffed animals) to reduce the demand that the kids find a mutually agreeable play idea in the moment.

Perhaps you pack a towel and a change of clothes, knowing that the morning dew will make the play equipment wet, and that your child cannot tolerate playing for long periods with even a drop of moisture on their clothes.

Do I need to drop demands, even if they are not hard for my child?

The short answer is yes, you may want to drop extra demands, even ones that may not look challenging for your child. By dropping a demand wholeheartedly and proactively, instead of the fake-drop, you are responding to your child with a needed accommodation.

Managing each demand costs your child nervous-system energy, (whether you see the cost or not) and when your child runs out of energy to manage demands, it's gone. The nervous system effort is cumulative. A child with no energy hits an adult with another expectation, kaboom! Big explosion! This may explain why your child seemingly explodes "over nothing" or "out of nowhere." By dropping extra demands, you increase capacity for those things that you choose to focus on and you align your child's energy with your true priorities.

As you work proactively, how can you communicate this decision to your children and your people so that it is no longer something you have to wonder about day by day?

As you work proactively, how can this dropped demand build trust, connection, and understanding?

When you drop extra demands, you build up their nervous system to sustain the impact of a larger demand, one that really matters.

For example, when we started occupational therapy intensively, we proactively dropped all sorts of demands at home that had become normal and acceptable—like choosing food with words, speaking kindly to brothers, and tolerating a less-desirable parent reading books at bedtime. We proactively dropped these demands by arranging for more support for brothers (playdates, time with grandparents) to separate them from potential verbal or physical explosions. We pulled out our printed menus for mealtimes and returned to meals made up of only his all-time favorite food choices. We communicated that only Mom would do books and snuggle him to sleep, so that he could count on this end to his day.

If you are just getting started, you likely do not know yet what your child's nervous system can handle. Perhaps you are seeing endless meltdowns and explosions, or you have a child heading toward or already in burnout. You may not yet have any clue what a life without all of this difficulty could look like.

Here's a new goal for you:

Create a positive set of expectations that your child can manage without explosions.

When we started, our son was in burnout, and my heart was breaking. I proactively and wholeheartedly dropped all sorts of expectations that he wasn't meeting anyway, but that I continued to hold onto. By using low-demand parenting, we created a set of positive expectations that he could meet. We wanted him to eat enough food to survive and to regulate. We wanted him to use his screen-time in his own way, for his own ends. We wanted him to use his alone time in his room for getting the space and healing he needed.

He was able to meet those expectations, day after day, and we used our energy on step 2 and step 5—figuring out what really matters, and getting our own needs met. Slowly, slowly, his nervous system regulated, receiving our affirming and understanding energy as healing. He did eventually emerge from his room. It felt endless; it felt terrifying, but low-demand parenting is what changed everything and put us on a different path forward.

> What about dropping demands for my neurotypical
> or non-explosive child? Do I need to drop demands
> even if they can handle them just fine?

I do not parent each of my kids the same way, but I do talk with them very openly about their brain types, the reality that we all need different things at different times, and that I will always meet them right where they are.

It is a family rule that we do not force each other; we ask. Our body, our choice. They know this, and so this means I drop demands when my child has difficulty with an expectation, regardless of their diagnoses. They know that I will not force them.

Jealousy is a type of difficulty, and by expressing jealousy or saying "It's not fair!", your child is offering meaningful communication that they may also be having trouble meeting some expectations or that they are still feeling forced and not feeling met. Any time I hear jealousy, I slow down to connect and listen to that specific child.

Is the issue really over this specific scenario, or has a challenging demand snuck in that I didn't notice?

Are they actually having some difficulty that I am not seeing?

When we are all feeling met and supported, right at our level of tolerance, we do not have much trouble with jealousy. It rises up, like all emotions do, and it resolves without needing more than emotional connection and validation.

* * *

5. Get creative in taking care of your own needs—without asking your child to do anything differently!

The real magic of low-demand parenting happens in the relationship that emerges between parent and child as you drop expectations, hold on to what really matters, and form new rhythms of communication and trust.

By dropping demands, it may feel at first as though you have just taken on a mountain of new demands for yourself. If you no longer ask your child to walk to the shoe bin and put on their own shoes independently, it may feel like you have to get them and put them on yourself.

So here's where you dig deeper into your creativity and your "why." If it feels like no big deal to put on their shoes yourself, then bingo, green light, keep going with it. That's an easy one.

If you feel rising resentment that you have to do this when your child is old enough and perfectly capable of doing it themselves, red light! This is a place to stop and dig. It's a can't, not a won't. But you have needs too, and the resentment is a sign that you have unmet needs.

So dig.

Why does putting on his shoes make you upset?

Because he's sitting there like a king demanding that I put on his shoes.

Why does him sitting there like a king upset you?

I have to run around everywhere finding the shoes and then putting them on him when I have my own stuff to be doing to get ready to go.

Ah-ha! An unmet need. You need to focus on yourself, but you can't because you have to put shoes on your child. This is helpful.

Let's dig more.

Why does putting on kid's shoes mean you can't focus on yourself?

Everyone is talking to me at once, and it's so stressful, and I can never find my keys when it's time to go. But if I make one wrong move my kid will explode.

Why is it so stressful?

We are always running late because I can't get my son to stop playing his game on his tablet, and I'm so focused on that that I can't keep track of the time.

Unmet needs for parent:

- help finding keys
- help with sound sensitivity
- help with keeping track of time
- help with the feeling of being late.

Challenging demands for kid:

- putting on own shoes to go somewhere
- stopping playing his game on tablet.

Creativity time!

Now there are literally hundreds of ways that your family could support these unmet needs and drop these challenging demands.

The key is to find something that lessens the burdens for you and actually makes life easier, instead of harder.

The secret sauce of low-demand parenting is the ease and flow that it brings into life, so the low-demand approach also needs to apply to the parent. If you simply ask more and more of yourself, you will burn out.

So here are some low-demand approaches to this situation:

- Don't ask kid to come at all. Is this an event they can skip?

- Don't go at all. Is this an event the whole family could skip?

- Don't ask kid to wear shoes to walk to the car. Can you remember to pop them in your bag on the way out the door?

- Don't ask kid to stop playing their game. Let them bring it with them. We adjusted our cell phone plan to one that includes unlimited data so that I can use my mobile hot spot in our van and anywhere that my child needs.

- Be late and take a deep breath.

- Start the "get ready routine" 10 minutes sooner mentally. If you usually start getting ready 15 minutes early, give it 25 minutes. To lessen the demand on you, set a phone timer or get Alexa to announce when its 25 minutes before soccer, or the next shoe-requiring event.

- Shift the "getting ready location" from some place noisy and crowded to someplace with more space. Can kids put on shoes outside the door instead of inside the door (where sound doesn't echo)?

- Can the rule about "no shoes in the house" be dropped so that there are not so many times that shoes need to go on and off?

- Can you get a "tile" or another key tracker to help support you in finding your keys?

- Can you get an extra key made to lessen the demand on you for finding them, or install a keyless entry system?

- Can a different adult in the family be responsible for finding keys before particular stressful events if you are the adult responsible for helping with shoes?

As you get creative in meeting your own needs without asking your child to do anything differently, you will truly unlock the magic of this system and set you and your child free to walk this path in confidence. As we explored above, demands are expectations layered over adult needs. When you take care of your own needs without layering expectations and demands on top, this low-demand approach begins to evolve into a sustainable lifestyle.

6. Create house rules

Can you make one decision that eases your daily life?

I lived in Brazil for a year in my 20s, a wild ride of cultural immersion in a language I'd never spoken before, without anyone I knew within a continent of me. I was decidedly alone. I spent a week in Rio de Janeiro on a homestay with a family who I met for the first time after a super early plane flight, and a particularly terrifying taxi ride through the twisty streets of Rio. "Never roll down your window," the cabbie barked at me in Portuguese, and though my stomach was rolling and there was obviously no AC, I held onto my seatbelt and survived the sweltering heat.

When I arrived at this family's house, they were just serving breakfast and asked me to sit down to eat with them. They served me first, platters of bread, cheese, bananas and avocado, which I politely made into a sandwich, with fruit on the side, salting my avocado and placing a slice of bread on top. I could feel the freeze in the room as they stared at my plate. I knew I did something wrong, but I had no idea what. I watched as every member of the family mashed their avocado with banana, sprinkling sugar on top, and then as they layered bread, jam, and cheese. There was a hidden expectation that no one shared with me, a right way to eat these breakfast items. An unwritten rule that avocado goes with sugar, not salt, and that it is never combined with cheese on a sandwich. I could've used some explicit house rules.

House rules bring unspoken demands into explicit, clear communication that all who enter your doors can follow.

Here are our family rules, all of which could be re-written as dropped expectations:

Rule 1—"We do not force or pressure one another. No means no, always. Your body, your choice."

Rule 2—"We give space when someone needs it."

Rule 3—"We can eat anything, anytime, anywhere. We listen to our bodies."

Rule 4—"We can choose when to use our screens without shame or limits."

Rule 5—"We are all always learning. When you're curious, uncertain or need help, just ask."

Rule 6—"We're doing our best, all on our own. We don't use punishments or rewards because we don't think they work."

Stating these as "family rules" takes the wondering out of it. I cannot suddenly decide that "screen-time is over" because that breaks our family rule, but I can ask my child if we can make a plan to play a game of Uno together this afternoon because it sounds fun to me.

Importantly, these rules apply to me too. If I don't like someone crawling on me, I remind them that it is my body, my choice, and if they need to snuggle, I can wrap them in pillows or snuggle them in a way that is more comfortable to my body. I get space when I need it, just like they do. I get to ask for help when I am uncertain. I am doing my best and do not need to be punished when I make a mistake.

These house rules are organized around a "can," not a "can't." So we do not have a house rule that says, "We keep each other safe," or "Hands are not for hitting," because these rules are essentially negation rules. The mere existence of a rule that limits freedom of expression (even through an undesirable medium like hitting) will increase nervous system activation and make it more likely that we will see stress behaviors like hitting. In other words, saying "We keep each other safe" is code for "We don't hit," but stating that makes it more likely that kids will hit. Instead, each of these rules is organized around a preservation and extension of autonomy, and I bring up these rules regularly as a reminder of each person's inherent autonomy in our household community. As such, their presence in our lives is a container. They are a supportive structure that ensures we will stay focused on what truly matters and continue to drop demands that are too much for us. They stretch us toward our family values of trust, autonomy, connection, and curiosity.

Admittedly, in the early days this is difficult work. But this intimacy and reciprocity grows as this new low-demand family culture takes root.

Chapter Six

———

How to Get Started with Low-Demand Parenting

START WITH FINDING A BIG DROP

Pick a category that doesn't matter to you, or where it's all "shoulds" and "good parents do X" and you're ready to be free.

> Maybe you decide that no one needs to wear clean clothes every day.
>
> Or maybe no one needs a bath except once a month.
>
> Or maybe you decide that popcorn and fruit roll ups will totally work as a dinner staple.
>
> Or you chop off someone's hair real short so there's no need to brush it.
>
> Or you release screen-time limits entirely.

Big drops will help you to move down the road because you decide once on a big topic, and then you get to enjoy the fruits of that one big choice.

FIND A MOTTO

While you are practicing low-demand parenting, it will be emotionally difficult. You have to do a lot of inner work to find out your why beneath these long-held demands. You will likely need to communicate with a partner, caregivers, or family to narrate your decisions. (I also give you permission to not explain yourself to others, to tell them what you are doing and leave it at that. I have some scripts you can use in the Resources section about low-demand parenting.)

Find a grounding motto that supports you as you move forward. Perhaps it is "My child deserves this support," or "Life will eventually get better," or simply "We are moving forward."

When we'd been stuck in endless meltdowns and so much aggression toward me and other siblings, it was hard to believe that anything would work. Every other strategy just made things harder. Just believing that this was worth it or would ever work took a monumental leap of faith. I was so desperate that I said to myself, "This has to work," which motivated me to jump in deeper, release more, and trust the process. You choose what words work for you.

A FAKE-DROP IS OK AT FIRST

Your child will be relieved and more well-regulated with every demand you can release. Just notice that you are faking it, and commit to the deeper work of investigating why, why, why, this matters. Reminder: a fake drop is when you release the demand but hold on to the underlying expectation that they be able do it.

WORK THROUGH YOUR DROPS IN REVERSE ORDER

Drop the things that don't matter to you first, and work on the deeper issues beneath the things that are really hard to let go of. It's worth it to find out why it matters so much and how you can let it go. You can do this, and it is hard.

Chapter Seven

Practical Examples

EXAMPLE 1—CEREAL MELTDOWNS IN THE MORNING

Problem

Your child is throwing cereal and screaming at his sibling at breakfast. You expect your child to sit and eat cereal with a spoon at the table with the rest of the family and the dog at the same time (this is actually a lot of expectations and you would want to list each one separately).

Demands

- Come downstairs

- Sit at the table in an adult-chosen chair

- Choose a cereal with words

- Wait for cereal to arrive

- Wait for milk to arrive

- Wait while milk is poured

- Eat cereal with an adult-chosen spoon

- Keep cereal on the table

- Tolerate other people talking while eating

- Tolerate a dog sitting next to chair while eating

- Carry bowl to sink when done

- Place it in the sink gently without clattering or breaking.

Do a big drop

What can you drop on this list that doesn't matter to you?

Can you drop the demand to come to the table and instead bring cereal to the child where they are already comfortable? (This eliminates many of these demands, but not all.) Can you drop the demand to eat at the same time and instead give the child their own time alone at the table?

Listen to what's hard

The adult sits down and says, "Sometimes it's hard to sit at the table with the family and the dog and eat cereal in the morning. I wonder what's hard about it..." and then you listen. Just listen. Maybe drawing or taking notes of what you hear. And then listen and listen and listen until the child has said everything they can possibly think of to say.

Remember: The point of the listening step is to discover demands that you didn't even see that are challenging at times for your child.

How we solved breakfasts

- We dropped the demand that our child eat at the table with the family or eat at a particular time.

- At first, this child needed total silence and alone time to eat breakfast, but also needed novelty of a new place to eat every day. So I set up a little pillow nest every day with stuffed animals, a blanket, and a tablet. It moved to a slightly different spot every day. I was willing and happy to do this because it meant we could have a calm morning, which was my top priority then.

- In the chaos of the mornings, I could not focus on meeting my struggling child's needs and those of my other two children, so I released my screen-time rules (screen-time limits was also a big drop that I did early on). That meant my other two kids could play Minecraft together, eating their preferred breakfasts too. When they were happy and satisfied, I could better meet my struggling kid's needs.

- I would bring a printed laminated menu with the six breakfast choices that I was committed to always having in the house (including "less healthy" options that my kid wanted to have on the menu, like Eggos). He could choose how he voted for his breakfast choice. He would write with a dry erase marker, point, use words, or put a toy on the chosen item, which helped offset the demand of the menu and only six set choices.

- Some days, the menu did become a demand and he would throw it or ignore it. On those days, I would bring all six items to him and set them up in front of him without speaking. He would point to what he wanted or knock over every item except the one he wanted.

- Once he'd eaten, he was able to speak, to engage and to work with me. But getting food in his body was an essential and challenging job, which is why I made it my first low-demand priority.

EXAMPLE 2—NOT TALKING TO US

Problem

Your child stops talking and ignores you, screams, kicks, punches, throws things, or rages instead.

Demands

- Listen to adult words

- Show that you heard adult words

- Process adult words in a certain amount of time
- Respond to adult words with your own mouth words
- Use "polite" mouth words
- Use "polite" tone of voice
- Avoid curse words.

Do a big drop

Drop "polite" as a family concept and drop any concerns with particular words. All words are ok now. Incorporate nonverbal communication for the whole family whenever possible (e.g., "Everyone who wants to go to the park can raise their hand!" instead of asking a question and requiring mouth words to answer).

Drop "in the moment"

Anytime your child seems to be getting stressed, you stop talking. Or greatly reduce your words. If you accidentally ask a question, say, "Oops, you don't have to answer that."

How we supported our son when words dropped out

When my son is calm, he is a chatter box, so it would have been easy to go with "shoulds"—he should be able to talk to me; he should be able to tell me what's hard; we should be able to talk this through kindly. But in our case, mouth words became impossible. They got stuck inside my child who wanted desperately to express his needs in words but could not. Again, it's a can't, not a won't. He either locked the door and ignored us completely, or raged and screamed, allowing this powerful communication to flow through his body and into the world.

I began to view his rages as meaningful communication and then could see his resilience, his fierce determination to be known. He did not play small in the world, and I was grateful.

But to ease the challenge of expression, we made communication boards for the toughest times of day and the hardest situations for him to talk. We made boards for him to say if he wanted to talk to me or be alone, if he was done talking or could keep going, how much energy he had in the tank, if he wanted Mom or Dad to be with him, and if he wanted food, water, or his tablet. Any time I was going to add a demand that he interact with me, I added in a nonverbal support so that he could use his native language to express himself.

Some of these nonverbal supports are in the Resources section.

EXAMPLE 3—REPAIR AFTER HOLDING A DEMAND YOU'D PREVIOUSLY DROPPED

Problem

My son was resisting going to speech therapy, which was rare for him. He loved the one-on-one attention and creative projects his therapist dreamed up. His resistance surprised me, and I thought I'd try pushing a little bit.

Demands

- Talk to mom about speech a second time
- Tolerate uncertainty about whether he would go
- Engage in a back-and-forth conversation
- Engage in a verbal conversation.

And then, if he did go to therapy, added demands would be:

- Leave our house
- Drive to therapy
- Walk into therapy
- Talk to the therapist about why he didn't want to come or listen while mom explains why he didn't want to come

- Discern in the moment if he wants to stay or when he wants to go.

Why it mattered to me

I believed he was making progress in speech, and I wanted the progress to continue. I personally really wanted him to go, because I get to sit and write in the waiting room, and I wanted a break.

What I did wrong

I pushed: "Today, it's a 'have to try'."

Kiddo wails: "Fine, fine! I'll go, you'll make me go, so I'll go." (An obvious sign of distress for him to is say, "Fine, I'll go." Quick deterioration to total meltdown.)

Me: "You don't have to stay if it doesn't feel right. We can leave any time." (Rapidly back pedaling—a drop in the moment.)

Kiddo, taking a breath: "But mom, you say we don't have any 'have to's'. But right now, you are foooooorcing me to go!!" (long wail)

Cue ah-ha moment for Mom!

What I realized

He's listening to me, and he knows our family culture.

He is holding me accountable to our house rules, that we don't have any "have to's" in our family. That if something is actually important to me, then I will make it a priority to slow down and work with my child ahead of time until it works for both of us.

What I did next

I needed to repair with my child: "You're so right buddy, we don't have any have to's. I messed up and I'm so sorry. I will not 'have to' you today. And thank you for reminding me. You're an amazing kid."

I learned again that I will not use my power over my child to get my needs met by demanding things of my child. I will not exert my will at the expense of my child's autonomy. My need for a break was real, but I got it in a different way. We agreed that he would watch an engaging YouTube video that he did not need me to watch with him, and I would walk laps around the block, waving to him at each lap. This worked for us both.

He went to speech happily the next week, but if he hadn't, that would've been ok too. That would be meaningful communication that there was a problem with speech, and I would have gone back to the method to be creative with next steps. I would have moved into the *why? why? why?* step to dig deeper into why this is important to me (or if it wasn't important anymore, I'd just drop it), and would have listened to my child with a genuine and gentle listening posture to learn more about what was leading to this difficulty.

It's ok to mess up and to get frustrated. It's ok to have your own needs. It's ok to wish this were easier. Perhaps you need to let yourself off the hook too. Being a low-demand parent means letting go where others hold on. It means letting go of the "shoulds" and the shame.

When you hold on to what really matters and let go of the rest, it is possible that it won't feel like letting go. It might feel like freedom.

———

Chapter Eight

Low-Demand Parenting and Screens

Screens and technology are kryptonite in so many families, that one area where low-demand feels too hard, the one place where parents put their foot down to insist that adults must keep control or else kids will spiral indefinitely. That may be true for your child. But as low-demand parents, we know that it's more about the path we take than the outcome at the end.

If a family arrives at screen-time boundaries after a thorough listening process to the caregiver's deep why and a collaborative listening process with the child; if it is a creative response that deepens trust between parent and child; if the adult's needs are taken care of without asking the child to do anything differently; if it expands a child's autonomy, then screen-time boundaries are a beautiful solution for that particular situation. Well done!

But if they are born from fear, based in control, and lead to battles between parents and children, then perhaps it's time to dig deeper.

Reframing your family's relationship to screens is all about the *process*, not the end *result*. We will move through the six steps of low-demand parenting to examine how you can craft your own unique low-demand approach to screen-time that works for your family.

Our story

Here's where we've ended up: I do not control my children's screen-time. They can have screen-time as often as they want, as long as they want, without judgment or shame.

If this means they watch YouTube for 12 hours a day, I will not shame them. If they want me to watch with them, I do. When they create a Minecraft world just to trap me in the dungeon, I wallow in the depths of despair in my virtual basement dungeon hell hole. When they want to talk to me about the latest Fortnite skins and exactly why Season Two, Episode Eight was the best yet, I listen and ask questions.

Important: I am not a gamer myself.

Of all of the passions on the earth that my children could choose, gaming would be on the bottom for me.

But my kids are hopelessly in love with video games. It turns out that I can truly love watching them play video games and can care deeply about enchantments, levels, powers, and bosses. Also, it turns out that it truly matters to them that I love and care deeply about their passions. Screen-time boundaries was one of my "big drops" early on—something I released early in the process because it was so necessary for my middle son Michael's healing from autistic burnout. He needed his screen to heal, but originally I was only "fake dropping" it. A fake-drop is when you drop the immediate demand but do not process the expectation or adult need beneath it. You drop the demand but not the underlying belief that it matters and that your child should be doing it. I fake dropped by allowing my child to go on watching endless YouTube, but I didn't do the deeper work around my own shame. I hid our struggle because of the way I was handling it.

I was afraid of judgment and knew that I could be accused of terrible parenting for "letting" my child sit in front of an iPad all day long.

It didn't feel like I was letting him do it; it felt like literally the only thing he could handle to do. Those YouTubers kept him company and connected with him when no one else could. Watching a British man assemble remote control cars in his workshop was meditative and restful for my exhausted, burned-out child. I could see the good in it, but would anyone else?

The fake drop was better than refusing to allow my son his chosen activity. At least I was not battling him, further deepening the void of trust, nor interrupting the cycles of healing. However, when I dug deeper into my shame, I realized that my fear of judgment was based on some loose definitions of "good parenthood" that crumbled under any scrutiny. *Good parents don't give their kids endless screen-time,* shouted the "shoulds." *But why?* I asked. *Because it's bad for them!* they shouted lamely.

But... but this isn't bad for my child. It doesn't look bad. It doesn't feel bad. He can't do anything else. What feels bad is the fear and the judgment.

If I let go of fear, I could meet my child with understanding and embrace him with compassion at his lowest moment.

This was my big drop. Dropping screen-time limits was so exhilarating because it was quickly clear that this was just the beginning of the transformation. As a choice steeped in shame, it felt like a leaping off of a cliff. But I began to wonder: If I wasn't controlling their screens, maybe I didn't need to control them at all. Maybe I could trust my children wholeheartedly. Maybe I could trust them to make their own right choices for right now. And that trust flung open my heart to simply show up as an astonished witness to another rich human life.

I've always felt the truest metaphor for parenting is being an orchestra conductor. My children were born playing certain instruments beautifully, with other instruments sitting dusty on the shelf. They were born to love to play certain songs. And as their orchestra conductor, my unique role is to help them play their chosen instruments to their chosen song.

Having been on a few more laps around the sun and having made a lot more mistakes than they have, I may have some wisdom to bear. But I have never lived their life nor seen the world from their eyes.

So, I hold them with open, trembling hands, humbly and reverently filled with gratitude. What a gift: I get to smell this freshly washed hair on this perfectly round head as this unique human snuggles up to me and asks me to play another game of Roblox.

One night recently, as I tucked my oldest son Owen into bed, he asked what I wrote about that day. I told him I was writing about why I do not limit screen-time, and his face lit up. "Yeah! And before you did that, we hardly had any at all!" he remembered. "Yup. It must have been a big change for you kids," I wondered aloud.

"Well..." Words began to flow as he caught his rhythm, "It felt like you stopped trying to control me. You listened to us, and the things we wanted to do were ok with you, and...and I was finally in charge of my own life. I like it when I can make my own choices, and screens are so good! They're not bad or evil or something. Imagine if I never found Fortnite! It's my favorite thing in the whole world!"

I saw the familiar expression of an autist whose brain is settling into thinking about their special interest. And I wondered—what if? What if I stayed on that path of control, hyper-fixation on doing the "right thing"? What if I continued to follow all the parenting rules that told me how to be "good"?

I would've missed this, I am sure, this specific joy of seeing my autistic children thrive in their own world where they make their own choices and love their own lives.

I would miss the chance to experience this free-flowing respectful conversation with my child who trusts me and tells me the truth. I would have missed the joy of being us.

WHY ARE WE ALL SO SCARED ABOUT SCREEN-TIME?

As a society, we have made major leaps with technology in a short period of time, which has led to a collective angst. Social scientists observe that with rapid changes in societal structures, communities offset this major transition by creating certain archetypical figures to absorb our uncertainty and our fears.[1]

Children's screen-time is just that archetypical focus for our fears.

To offset our own concerns with broad rapid societal changes in technology, we have collectively latched onto the impact of screens on children. This is not a new or novel process. It repeats in every generation. Playing card games,[2] watching cartoons[3]—these things seem fairly innocuous now, but they were intensely loaded, explosive topics for parents in their time.

So, you are not alone in being concerned with screen-time, nor are you making this up. You have been fed this fear, and it has been intensely reinforced. This context makes it very hard to do the sort of honest introspection and creative out-of-the-box thinking that is that hallmark of low-demand parenting. So, if this is particularly hard for you, it makes sense.

In addition, as with so many areas where our needs can be disordered and addictive, screen-time use can become a significant challenge for adults and children, and can require specially trained professional support to find controlled ways to use it.[4] If you suspect a true addiction, as with all approaches to addiction, bravely face the temptation to shame yourself or your child, and instead embrace the reality that addiction is a mental health symptom, a sign of a struggling and suffering human, who is beautiful and whole. Seek

---

1   See the concept of "bridezilla" in Rebecca Mead's *One Perfect Day: The Selling of the American Wedding*. New York: Penguin Books, 2008.

2   Irving Crespi, "The Social Significance of Card Playing as a Leisure Time Activity." *American Sociological Review 1967, 21(6)*. https://www.jstor.org/stable/2088423.

3   Ladislaus Semali, *Literacy in Multimedia America: Integrating Media Education Across the Curriculum*. Abingdon: Routledge Library Editions, 2000.

4   Manoj Kumar Sharma and Thamil Selvan Palanichamy, "Psychosocial interventions for technological addictions," *Indian Journal of Psychiatry 2018*, Feb. https://www.ncbi.nlm.nih.gov/pmc/articles/PMC5844169/

professional support, while prioritizing a trusting connection with your child. There are many theories and approaches to screen-time addiction, and you can use a low-demand approach with providers to determine the best path forward.

For the purpose of low-demand parenting, we are going to act as though screens are morally neutral. We are going to set aside the wider culture's conviction that screens for children is something loaded and intense, of ultimate importance, the ultimate evil.[5] Instead, we are going to treat it like any other decision, where there is not one "right answer" but rather there is a process to land at the right decision for your family, for this moment in time.

SCREENS AND ADULT SHAME

Despite the many headlines declaring that pandemic children have more screen-time than ever and the apparent understanding that adults with full-time jobs simply cannot also provide full-time entertainment and stimulation, there is more than enough screen-shame to go around.[6] Shame is a complex and painful emotion that thrives unspoken, in secrecy and darkness.[7] Shame says that if we break the codes of good parenthood, we are bad and do not deserve love or connection.

When I first released my tight hold around screen-time, I didn't know who to tell. It was a major change in our family culture, but would anyone understand? Or would they simply judge me as a lax,

---

5   See the American Academy of Pediatrics, "Policies on Children and Media," https://www.aap.org/en/patient-care/media-and-children/policies-on-children-and-media/

6   Matt Richter, "Children's Screen-time Has Soared in the Pandemic, Alarming Parents and Researchers," *New York Times*, Jan 16, 2021. https://www.nytimes.com/2021/01/16/health/covid-kids-tech-use.html

7   Brene Brown, "Shame." "Connection, along with love and belonging (two expressions of connection), is why we are here, and it is what gives purpose and meaning to our lives. Shame is the fear of disconnection—it's the fear that something we've done or failed to do, an ideal that we've not lived up to, or a goal that we've not accomplished makes us unworthy of connection. *I'm unloveable. I don't belong.*" Brene Brown, *Atlas of the Heart: Mapping Meaningful Connection and the Language of Human Experience*. New York: Penguin, 2021, 135–140.

permissive parent, taking the easy road by slapping my children in front of screens so I could scroll Instagram in peace?

Who would witness the miracle that was unfolding in our household as I released my hold over this elusive anchor of "good parenthood"? As I stopped trying to control my children's passions and instead welcomed in their favorite activity and greatest delight?

Who would celebrate with me? I no longer battled with my children every day. Instead, I was learning to show up for them no matter what they chose, no matter how socially acceptable or unacceptable it might be. One of the greatest joys of my life was unfolding right before my eyes, the chance to partner with my children in creating a good life of their choosing for their flourishing.

I felt I couldn't share this transformation with my friends, family, and the world because of shame.[8] Screen-time decisions are deeply entrenched in shame. Many parents hide their children's screen-time and shame themselves for their decisions, regardless of what they are. In light of the intense collective fear surrounding screens, this shame makes sense.

To embrace something our culture has decided is the ultimate evil...how can that decision be celebrated? And yet it can! We must name this shaming if we are to be free to make wise choices.

SCREENS AND CHILDREN'S SHAME

I knew that screen-time was becoming a source of shame for my kids because they were sneaking it, stealing technology, and hiding in their closets to use it. They blamed and shamed each other: "All you love is screen-time," as though this delight in their lives was something icky and awful.

Any time the house got quiet, I knew they'd stollen my phone and were sneaking in a bit of game playing or YouTubing.

So, we created a house rule around screens:

---

8 "Shame thrives on secrecy, silence, and judgment," Brene Brown, *Atlas of the Heart: Mapping Meaningful Connection and the Language of Human Experience.* New York: Penguin, 2021, p.137.

"We can choose when to use our screens without shame or limits."

This opened up conversation about shame, how it leads us to hide, to sneak, and to worry that we are bad for the choices we make. I got to tell my precious little ones that they never need to hide their passions and loves from me, no matter how different they may seem.[9]

"All of you is safe with me," I said, thinking ahead to teenage years and adulthood when these small people will be big, with the freedom to decide whether they will trust me with their secrets or not, whether they will come to me when life comes crashing down, or not.

By naming shame early, and rooting out these corrosive beliefs that the things they loved made them bad, my hope is that when their loves and passions get bigger, they will continue to trust me to hold it without shaming them.

The other great gift is that I am no longer screen-time police. We do not fight each other. I do not have to boss them around.

When we have a stop time, like to go to therapy or grandma's house, we are a team figuring out the best way to stop. Together, we tackle the problem. Together, we find a solution. We high-five, celebrating our shared skills at managing challenging events, united.

To be a team with my children is worth all the judgment in the world.

That is why this is a hill I would die on, because the gifts of shame-free partnership with my children are richness beyond compare.

---

9   "If we're willing to dare greatly and risk vulnerability with each other, wor-thiness has the power to set us free," Brene Brown, *Daring Greatly: How the Courage to be Vulnerable Transforms the Way We Live, Love, Parent and Lead*. New York: Penguin, 2012, p.10.

Chapter Nine

A Low-Demand Approach to Screens

1. PUT WORDS TO THE DEMAND ITSELF

Step one is about identifying the demands so that you can proactively drop them. Naming these demands is a process in itself. You may start with the big issue of "screens" and then dig down deeper into all the tiny demands nestled within the one big one. Get specific about the context and treat each context as a unique demand. The demand to stop playing Minecraft to go to occupational therapy will be different than the demand to stop watching YouTube to play at the park.

Screen-time demands largely fall into several categories:

- Overall limits on amount of time (like a specific time of day, an amount of time per day)

- Limits on content (acceptable games or apps, content that kids can access on YouTube)

- Transitioning from technology to other events

- Demands internal to games themselves (managing challenges, spending money).

Write down as many demands as you can, including ones that your child seems to be handling just fine (you can celebrate those successes and also keep in mind that in some seasons we have to pull back on "easy-demands" to accommodate a bigger priority ask).

Use the guide in the Resources section. Be as specific as possible. If you just write "stopping the screen," you will not get where you want to go. Each situation is different, and solvable, and the more specific you are, the easier it gets. Use these questions to find as many demands as you can.

✳ ✳ ✳

2. FIND OUT WHY THIS MATTERS TO YOU

Your "why" is the *most* important part of this process. It may take time to get to the true why for these demands related to screen-time, or it may not. My "why" turned out to be entirely based on fear, so once I released the fear, the old why evaporated and I was able to dig into a new why.

My new, positive "whys" for screens are:

Release shame

Celebrate passion

Explore in freedom

Create space for connection.

Release shame

No shaming me or my kids for our screen-time choices. This means I do not read articles (even ones lovingly sent) about the harmful effects of screen-time. These do not align with my deep why because they lead me into places of shame.

Celebrate passion

At the same time as I release shame, I am also careful with how I speak about my children's screen-time choices, ensuring I am publicly celebrating their passions and accomplishments, including beating a boss level or logging a certain number of hours. If we are to live without shame, we get to embrace the things that make us come alive, including when those things happen on a screen.

Explore in freedom

When things come up that are unexpected and which trigger fear for me (like violence, objectification of women, curse words), I consider it an opportunity for us to explore this thing together. It was going to come up because it is a part of the world. I know about it, which is something to celebrate, and my child is open to talking to me, also a gift not to be squandered. We have had incredible conversations about each of these topics, and my kids are now empowered with both my opinions and their own to navigate the digital complexities of our modern world. Open, accepting, shame-free conversation is amazingly powerful.

Create space for connection

I play *with* my kids in their games, and I use their preferred technology to connect with them. Sometimes it is easier to have a conversation about anxiety with my nine-year-old over a Google Meet call than face-to-face in real life. Sometimes texting emojis is a way to reconnect with Michael after a meltdown. I encourage grandparents to download Roblox and play with their grandkids for a few minutes, even though they'd probably rather snuggle and read a book. The point is to connect, and we have to start by connecting on the kid's terms before we ask them to connect on ours. Technology provides us a beautiful opportunity to do exactly that.

Before I make any demands of my child, I weigh them against my "why"—does it release shame, celebrate my kid's passion, enable us to explore our freedom together and/or create space for connection? If so, it's aligned with my deep why. If not, I have some work to do to ensure that this is still a demand that I feel comfortable prioritizing.

What is your deep why for screens?

Why do your demands for screens matter to you? And why does that truly matter? And why does that truly matter? We keep pressing into the why until our body responds because that is a good sign that we have gotten to the root of the truth.

If your deep why is grounded in fear, see if you can turn it around into a positive statement of what you do want to see or that you do believe. You may want to ask, "What do I hope my child will learn by my letting go of this specific screen-time demand?"

Examples

By letting go of a limit around certain games—I hope my child will learn that I trust him to explore new things and decide for himself if they feel good or not.

By letting go of a time limit—I hope my child will learn to regulate using all the tools available, including screen tools, and that she will also learn to know when she needs a different type of tool, like playing outdoors.

By letting go of the rule of no screens at the table—I hope my child will find our family table to be a safe and accommodating environment.

Remember that the "why" step is to determine those core values that you want to hold onto, while dropping the expectation. You can continue to believe in the power of outdoor learning while still supporting your child's choice to read on a tablet indoors.

Two things can be true at the same time.

When my real why is fresh air, I realize that I can open all the windows in a room even if my child doesn't leave that room. We can listen to our audiobooks outside with the sun on our faces. We can play their favorite games "in real life" by digging up the yard like Minecrafters or chasing each other around with Nerf guns like Fortnite or doing tasks all over the house like Among Us (this is our favorite way to knock out our household jobs!). Because I have played all these games with them on their devices, I know how to translate them into real life and how to weave them into my other priorities like getting vigorous exercise, having sensory-immersive play, and contributing to the household community.

* * *

3. LISTEN TO YOUR CHILD

This step is so crucial for a low-demand approach to screens. In the listening step, we listen deeply and exhaustively to our children to discover additional demands that we can drop proactively. We listen for their unique perspective, allowing them to rework our preconceived ideas. This is particularly important when it comes to screens, as our children's perspective on them is often very different than our own. We were not raised in the same world as they were. This is ok; it is important to name. When it comes to technology, they have perspectives, wisdom, and experience that we can only guess at.

For example, my son was exploding regularly while using his tablet, and it was driving me crazy. I had all my usual thoughts of banning technology from the household, restricting his time, and wishing I'd never introduced my children to video games in the first place.

But instead, I asked for more information after one specific explosion (when he had calmed down). He explained that this one particular game was really fun until one day he got to a certain level, and it became impossible. I asked if I could look more closely and discovered that the difficulty had been accidentally set to "ultra," and when we ratcheted it back to "medium," it was fun again.

The problem wasn't with the technology or the amount of time he was spending. The problem was that he can't read and accidentally clicked a button. I was able to solve the problem quickly and get him back to happily enjoying his game.

This seems simple and obvious. But it surprises me how often we adults forget to slow down and listen to our children. You may be seeing a meltdown when it's time to come eat dinner and blame it on the fact that they can't stop watching Netflix. But with a good discussion, it becomes clear that the dinner table is boring, and they hate the ritual of answering questions about their day. The right demands to drop would be answering questions and of sitting through lengthy conversations at dinner, neither of which have anything to do with screens.

Remember to do your own work around shame and screens before coming to your child. Even if they are young, they have likely absorbed some of our wider culture's ambivalence about screen-time. They see adults glued to their phones on sidewalks, in the pickup line, and in the grocery store, and yet they also know that kids are not supposed to love technology, that it is somehow shameful, and that they might be bad for loving it.

Depending on the limits you've had in the past and the messages you've implicitly or explicitly sent about screen-time, they may not be willing to talk to you about it at all. Kids sense our energy deeply and are always scanning to see if they are safe. Shame is a corrosive emotion that thrives in secrecy. Even a whiff of shame and your child may shut down (or explode at you).

You may not be able to have any productive conversations about screens until after you have taken on a low-demand approach for long enough to fully convince them that you support this choice. As their parent or caregiver, it is important to recognize that your child is reading your nonverbal and energetic signals more than your explicit verbal ones.

Even a year after I explicitly made the move to drop limits and embrace screen-time, Michael would continue to taunt his brothers saying, "All you ever want to do is play with screens!" as though this were a bad thing. Even though I regularly reminded him that we support screen play in our family, he held onto a kernel of shame. Only after 18 months of shame-free screen usage has this habit finally evaporated.

4. WORK PROACTIVELY TO DROP DEMANDS

As you work proactively, how can you communicate this decision to your children and your people so that it is no longer something you have to wonder about day by day?

As you work proactively, how can this dropped demand build trust, connection, and understanding?

Our proactive house rule:

"We can choose when to use our screens without shame or limits."

You will want to create your own proactive plan to drop demands and embrace your deep why. Is it maintaining your daily routine with screen-time limits, but allowing screens at the table? Is it dropping the limits around what games are considered safe, while increasing the amount of time you spend playing those games with your child so that you understand them and can talk with your child about them? Do you want to drop time limits all together, while supporting yourself emotionally? Perhaps you could access this support by reading from the Resources section and surrounding yourself with other adults who support your decision to counteract any possible shame?

The point is to define the demands, even the little, tiny ones, figure out why you are enforcing those demands and why they matter, listen to your child, and then drop as many as you can to bring stability to your household.

Being proactive will bring you the greatest freedom. Explain your deep why to your children and bring them in on your choice. It's a great moment to share a transformation in your own thinking. Your children will get a sense of what it looks like for an adult to change their mind.

Screens give you an opportunity to practice dropping even small demands that your child may be able to sustain, but by dropping them you build them up for larger demands. When you drop extra demands, you build up their nervous system to sustain the impact of a larger demand, one that really matters.

For example, if your priority is to ease the transition to bedtime with fewer meltdowns, you may drop the adherence to stopping screens at a specific time. If you normally require them to stop at a set time, try discussing a new plan —that you've noticed that it's hard to stop in the middle of a video, and you've got a new idea. What if they finished their video, their game, or their show instead, and then you head to bed after that? Share that your top priority is to transition to bedtime smoothly and ask if this plan will help. Do they have any more ideas for ways to transition smoothly to bedtime? You might be surprised what they have to share.

You can practice stopping, making it a game, perhaps asking them to be the grown-up and you be the kid, allowing you to playfully bring up some of the potential pitfalls to this arrangement. You can insist on one more video and change your mind about which one is the last one. See what your "grown-up" does!

In the moment, if your child cannot stop, the low-demand approach is to say "ok." In the moment, we choose connection and release expectations. This is a sign to continue to work proactively, to check in with your why (is a set bedtime your singular top priority for the day? If so, why does this particular bedtime matter to you?), to listen to the child's concerns, and to drop as many other demands as possible to support this top priority demand.

* * *

5. GET CREATIVE IN TAKING CARE OF YOUR OWN NEEDS WITHOUT ASKING YOUR CHILD TO DO ANYTHING DIFFERENTLY

When we first dropped screen-time limits, my children were so excited (and so dysregulated), that it initially looked like months of pure screen-based exploration. As already stated, video games are not my jam. I was bored (and scared), and I wanted my children to make different choices to better accommodate me and my needs. I almost took back the decision to remove limits many times, simply because I wasn't satisfied with our daily life. Once I recognized this, I was able to appreciate that this was my problem and that I did not need to ask my kids to do anything differently. I could solve it on my own.

I began my search for hobbies that I could do while sitting next to a child watching a video on YouTube. I found good ear plugs that filtered out the tinny noise of the games while allowing my children's voices to come in without any trouble. I invested in a Kindle so it would also keep my page marked and I could keep it in my pocket. I tried crochet and knitting. I experimented with drinking lots of kinds of tea. Eventually I discovered my old love of writing. Prayers, blog posts, and book chapters flowed from my fingertips as I sat next to my children, creating Minecraft masterpieces. I calmed my fears, accepted where my kids were and what they needed, and solved my own problem.

I also surrounded myself mentally with sources of support for this approach because I knew I was vulnerable to shame and judgment on hard days. I listened to podcasts and read supportive resources. I made the decision not to second-guess my choice by clicking on those judgmental articles and held these same boundaries with extended family.

The only-screens phase lasted longer than I wanted. I wanted them to get their fill and then intrinsically decide to shift toward creative outdoor play within a month or two. But the months stretched on, and it was challenging for me and my husband. I realized that this meant it was a type of fake-drop. Fake-dropping demands is when you drop the immediate demand but not the underlying belief that it matters and that your child should be doing it. I dropped the demand that my children spend much of their time outdoors, but I hadn't probed deeply into the belief that it matters, and that my children should be doing it. I was holding onto a belief that my children should be outside instead of inside watching videos about kids playing outside.

Gently, steadily, I let this belief go.

Eventually, I was able to recognize that being outside is extremely important *for me*. I can share my love of outdoors with them, but I cannot make them love it too. My children are unique, distinct from me, with their own path to walk.

Just because something is important to me does not necessarily make it important to them.

I installed a swing on our patio and cleaned up our comfy outdoor sofas. I communicated that it was important to me to spend time in the swing, outdoors, every day. I sat in my swing and read my book, and soon children wandered out, iPads in hand, to sit with me on the sofa. From there, we had a launching point for invitations to tag, neighborhood kids riding scooters, and a chance to hop in my swing or get pushed on the swing set. Creating a middle ground space—a comfy space to use screens outside—made the transition possible.

6. USE NOVELTY

This is the easiest step when it comes to screens because novelty is inherently built into the digital life. It is always new! Games have new levels and new updates. New YouTube videos come out every day. The stock of audiobooks from the library is endless and at your fingertips. So instead, learn from and lean on these sources as you support your child's love of novelty. Watch your child engage on their device, and if they can tolerate it, comment on the ways that they are self-regulating.

My son gets bored with certain videos and switches them off in the middle. I may observe later, "When you were watching that YouTube video about engines, I saw the way you noticed that you were getting bored and made a different choice without even getting upset! I wonder how you knew you were bored?"

Where we are now

Coming up on two years without externally-imposed screen-time limits, my children have found their own paths, each journey as unique as the child. Nine-year-old Owen did loads of research and eventually graduated to a full gaming PC where he can take his love of complex gaming to the next level. He makes loads of friends online and is achieving true mastery in his games. He knows when he wants a break and often opens the windows in his room to get fresh air while he plays.

Seven-year-old Michael starts his day with YouTube, plays Minecraft to connect with his brothers, and otherwise wants to spend his day crafting, building obstacle courses, and taking walks. He uses his screen-time to decompress after difficult encounters that tax him, and as a safety net in environments where he is uncomfortable or when he is bored.

Five-year-old Leo has learned complex math from a British tv show and loves to take videos of himself showing off his toys like a YouTuber. But he would typically rather be playing with friends, heading to school, swinging, or soundly beating an adult in Uno. He loves to play Roblox to connect on equal footing with Owen, despite their four-year age difference, and escapes to the safety and predictability of YouTube videos when Michael explodes on him.

I am proud that they are learning now what many adults still haven't learned—how to regulate their own screen-time usage in line with their body's needs, their many interests, and the variety of ways we connect through technology.

From these early ages, we are engaging in meaningful discussion about tech usage and healthy habits. They witness my husband and I making our own unique decisions about screen-time usage as we each use computers as the basis for our work. We have an open dialogue about what to do if you see something that scares or confuses you, and have many conversations as a family about how to tell fact from fiction online. This digital literacy flourishes in a low-demand, shame-free environment.

WHAT IS THERE TO LOVE ABOUT SCREEN-TIME?

Creativity, autonomy, and freedom

When kids are engaged with technology, they are in full control. They can control the volume (unlike when the music is too loud in the grocery store). They can switch videos immediately when one is too boring (unlike when waiting for Mom to finish a boring phone call). They can ban a fellow player who doesn't obey the rules (unlike on the playground when that kid can just run up and try to play again). They can investigate every minute interest on YouTube with a community of other people who are also obsessed with that particular Pokémon (unlike in real life when people tune out the 15th time).

Particular games and activities for particular feelings/emotions

"Screen-time" is not a monolith, nor are video games. Checking out audio books from the library on their tablets gives my non-readers access to endless books delivered in ways they can understand. YouTubers who do read-aloud books help when Mom is too busy to read at that exact moment. Voice dictation gives a feeling of independence and mastery when you can't write. Music and having YouTube on in the background give extra stimulation when kids are building with Lego or doing a sensory bin. Taking pictures and editing videos is a joint project, bringing out opportunities for collaboration and creative expression. Calming meditation apps or fidget apps can replace fidget toys when a person is overstimulated.

And then there's the huge range of video games! Zelda is for adventuring and exploring. YouTube is for vegging, TikTok is for fast-paced entertainment, and Fortnite is for connecting and collaborating with online friends; Roblox is for seeing quick progress and feeling powerful; Minecraft is for slow growth and creative expression. And also for trapping Mom in dungeons.

A controlled environment

If my kids are battling in a video game, one can leave the game to show their disagreement with the way the other is playing. This is much harder to do in real life, especially when you are on the receiving end of another person's aggression. We can turn on controls in games like putting Minecraft into "peaceful" instead of "hard" to find that just right challenge level. We can put in supports so that dying in the game doesn't mean losing all your hard-won inventory.

Translatable problem-solving skills

The wisdom of video games helps us solve real life problems. We can create "check points" so if you mess up, you can "respawn" and get a do-over. We can monitor our "hearts" and notice when we're getting low. We can start easy and "level up" once we're feeling confident.

Social and relational skills

Online friendships involve just as much learning and socializing as in-person ones, and my kids are both challenged and connected in their virtual friendships. By using headphones and engaging with other kids in a game, they have a chance to navigate challenging situations with me literally at their side. We have co-navigated what to do if a kid is bullying them, if someone uses words they don't like, or if a kid is just not fun to play with. They can mute and talk it through with me in real time.

The opportunity to offer grace

The world does not end if a kid gets so frustrated that they throw and break the tablet. No meaningful life lessons have to be learned from our worst, most impulsive and dysregulated mistakes.

DOCUMENT THE LEARNING

I encourage you to watch your child using technology and write down everything they are learning, everything you can support, every way that they are developing into the little people you want them to be. You can use the guide in Resources section to document this learning, and you'll probably want to add to it all the time, as they are always learning, growing, and developing new skills. Get ready to be blown away!

Chapter Ten

Our Story of Low-Demand Co-Parenting

OUR STORY

A few years ago, my partner Brian and I crossed the line where now we have been dating or married for longer than we haven't. We have been traveling life's journey together for longer than we were apart.

Like any couple who've been together a long time, we have grown up together, changed together, and been through our own challenges, together.

When arriving at low-demand parenting, we came with our own stories, our own family backgrounds, our own dreams, and our own work to do internally to reckon with the path our parenting journey had taken.

Neither Brian nor I expected parenting to be quite so hard.

Babies

Our first child Owen was smiley, engaging, and hilarious, a big personality from the start. Incredibly precocious and intelligent, he began speaking in complete sentences when he could barely walk and loved to take control of a room as a toddler, directing the minute actions of every adult like a tiny blond drill sergeant. He was our first child, and we were smitten.

We also recognized early that this boy was off the charts sensitive. Physically, emotionally, intellectually, sensorially—he was deeply attuned to the world around him. Owen required exacting parenting. Everything had to be exactly-so to avoid a meltdown. We heated his towels in the dryer for exactly five minutes to ensure he could get out of the bath. We adjusted his shoes endlessly until they were exactly right. We read the same books, rocked him in our arms in a pitch-black room, and walked out the door at 7pm on the dot. We were a finely tuned trio. Two highly attuned parents aligned with a challenging and delightful little one.

And then we had another baby.

Like many families of neurodivergent, highly sensitive, and gifted children, our second child Michael changed everything. We did our best to maintain total stability for Owen and were so grateful that Michael seemed to require nothing more than to sleep in his car seat. Michael wanted to be left alone, while Owen required our total and complete attention. Michael had major gastroesophageal reflux disease (GERD), which impacted every aspect of his life with terrible discomfort and delayed his motor development. But soon enough Michael wanted to crawl, touch, and grab, and this disrupted all of Owen's finely tuned routines. Owen responded with more control. He insisted that we dress them exactly alike, down to the socks and underwear, and so I purchased everything in twos, like twins, sliding underwear over Michael's little diaper so that they would be exactly alike, to Owen's exacting specifications.

As co-parents, we were holding on. Our family system was shaped around Owen's stability and Michael's health concerns. Routines kept us moving. When we got time to sleep and talk and connect, we spent most of the time talking about our children. We knew that our parenting experience was unusual, but we had not yet accepted just how far off the traditional path we were straying. "Everyone is exhausted, right? Everyone is struggling, right?" We asked the questions. We did not know the answers. We looked to our friends for validation, but their kids seemed impossibly easy by comparison. "What are we doing wrong?" we asked. But our sample size was so small, just a few friends, a few kids.

We also knew that we were not processing at the same pace. I intuitively accepted our children's uniqueness, likely because of my own then-undiagnosed neurodivergence. I rebelled against coercive parenting methods because of how hard it was for me as a child to bear even my parents' disappointment. But I also struggled to create routines that worked for our complex family of four.

Brian was less comfortable with our children's differences and held onto the belief that they were normal and our parenting was to blame. He believed that with clearer routines, responsibilities, and boundaries, they could meet our expectations. He was also working very long hours, impossibly stretched between home and work.

For my part, I struggled to trust Brian with decision-making. I micro-managed and controlled the family's decisions without listening well or even consulting him at times. Powerless and concerned, he disengaged.

And then we had another baby.

Three boys in four years

This time, it all fell apart. Our system could not bear the impact of another baby. I developed postpartum depression. Brian went underwater too, drowning in the dual demands of work stress and home stress, as he was stretched beyond his breaking point. Four-year-old Owen's meltdowns got more aggressive and explosive. He banged his head on walls and became unable to tolerate any clothing on his body. I watched him fall asleep naked with tears drying on his cheeks, my ears ringing from his screams.

At age two, Michael finally began to babble but with a significant speech impediment so no one but me could understand him. His aggression toward other children on the playground meant I could never be more than arm's length away from him. His health concerns continued. He struggled to nap, constantly interrupted by baby Leo's cries. I moved Owen and Michael into the same room, where I discovered after a nap time that Owen had pulled every book off his bookshelf and piled them around Michael, who sat covered in books, shrieking.

As co-parents, we were never farther apart than in those early days of having three boys in four years. We loved each other fiercely, and when talking about anything other than our children or work, we still aligned easily. But those two topics were so incredibly loaded that we edged up to them and around them, fighting to stay connected despite these wedges that drove us apart. Naturally, lack of sleep helped nothing.

We limped around these fractures, healing in our own ways. Brian got his dream job with the accompanying pressure to succeed, while settling into his joy and satisfaction in a career he loved. I discovered my neurodivergence while addressing my mental health needs and trauma history. Our children grew older, and their needs grew more complex.

It is a steep challenge to remain close emotionally and practically with another human. We wove in and around one another in those days, sewing seeds of trust and distrust, connection and alienation. We disagreed openly, and we disagreed silently. We avoided looking too closely at certain topics for fear of provoking a serious examination. We aligned and smiled and laughed and went on vacation and went out to dinner. Life isn't a neat and tidy story.

Stepping off the mainstream path

It wasn't until Owen's anxiety became debilitating and Michael refused to attend school in any form that I realized I was ready to step out of mainstream parenting all together. I wanted an entirely different approach, one that took the needs and struggles of our kids seriously but didn't leave me feeling like a failure as a parent. I knew this was what I needed, and I had a strong hunch it was what our kids needed. I did not think it was a plan that Brian would immediately agree with. I did it anyway.

My first big drop was our screen-time limits, a decision I made unilaterally because I wasn't willing to enforce them (along with the subsequent battles). I dropped the expectation that Owen complete all his virtual school assignments, choosing an unschooling approach instead. Michael was experiencing autistic burnout and spent hours alone in his room. I chose not to pressure him to rejoin the family, instead respecting his process and delivering bowls of pretzels in silence.

Little Leo would not let me out of his eyesight, preferring that we were touching at all times. I sat beside this boy, who had experienced substantial trauma in his early years, and watched hours of dancing numbers singing songs and sat through endless episodes of pajamaed superheroes saving the day. I was not allowed to do anything besides watch with him—at times he even held my face to his cheek to ensure I watched—and I allowed this. He began sleeping in my bed at night, a move we'd never taken with our other kids. I moved his bed to sit right by mine and invested in a larger bed to accommodate his nightly choice to snuggle me while he survived his nightmares.

Meanwhile, my beloved co-parent was struggling. He saw my choices and did not outright challenge them, but could not see where this would lead and could not explicitly support me. I accepted his limits and the level of support he could offer without bitterness. I sought to undo my longstanding pattern of pushing him to the margins of our shared life if he didn't agree with me. Brian showed up and shared his thoughts, even when he wasn't sure I would care. I fought hard to listen to his concerns and to look for solutions we could all live with, solutions that satisfied his deep needs while not asking the kids to do anything differently. Brian worked on his powers of introspection, to land on his own true concerns and to bravely put words to these deep needs.

This season required us to use our low-demand skills on all fronts at once—with ourselves, with each other, and with the kids.

It's a can't, not a won't

I discovered early that I could not simply ask more and more of myself or I would burn out. The same was true of my partner. I could not ask more and more of him, or our relationship would fracture.

I could not expect him to be where I was or to agree with me all the time. When he didn't agree or didn't align or needed more time, it wasn't that he wouldn't support me. *It was that he couldn't.* He was doing the best he could and wanted to support me as much as he could. I had to extend the same grace to my husband as I was learning to offer our kids (and myself!). I needed to learn to see the demands I was placing on him that were too hard and to learn to practice low-demand partnering.

Along the way, he discovered his intrinsic abilities to practice a low-demand lifestyle and his own natural joy as he began to extend the same grace to me. Our relationship grew by leaps and bounds as we let each other off the hook more and expected less.

Chapter 11 explains how we did it.

Chapter Eleven

A Low-Demand Approach to Co-Parenting

1. PUT WORDS TO THE DEMAND ITSELF

I adapted to low-demand parenting seamlessly. It just fit. But for my partner, it required a lot of work—both internal processing and practical shifts. It is very common among low-demand parents for one partner to adopt the philosophy more quickly and easily, and for the other to have more difficulty.

Brian was immensely brave to learn, to change, and to do the deeper work. I was brave to strike out in a new direction without my partner by my side, and to give him space to join me in his own time, and in his own way.

Regardless of where you are coming from, you will need your courage. This journey is ultimately about the best things in life: freedom, connection, vulnerability, and joy. But there is hard work to do to get there. The truth is that we are demand factories for our partners, just like we are for our kids. Maybe more so! It may be harder to identify these demands, but it is crucial to slow down and spend time on this step to truly move into a low-demand approach to your partner.

You may not need to write down every demand and investigate the deeper why in each situation. But taking the time to see yourself honestly will develop your lens in the relationship with your partner.

How to see the demands

Here are some prompts to begin to look at the demands you are making of your partner in relation to your co-parenting:

- What do you wish they would do that they never do?

- What do you have to ask of them over and over?

- Where do you think your partner is wrong and you are right?

- What topics bring up resentment between you?

- If you could wave a magic wand and change one thing about co-parenting with your partner, what would it be?

- When you are stressed with your kids, what do you try to control about your partner?

As I began this journey, the philosophy of Al Anon supported me. Al Anon is a worldwide collective of family members of alcoholics, and though this isn't my story, the wisdom of this community moved me deeply. A core philosophy of Al Anon is to release expectations:

> Expectations are the breeding ground for anger and resentment and the potential for suffering when my expectations are not met. I can poison my relationships when I continually try to change others to meet my expectations.[1]

Demands are the tip of the iceberg, and layered underneath are our expectations, those positive things that we wish our spouse would do. Beneath our expectations are our needs. This is where we are vulnerable, and this is where we must become honest.

Co-parenting examples

Demand: Let our child eat in his room instead of at the dinner table.

---

1   The Al Anon Forum Magazine, book 3, March 2020, al-anon.org.

Expectation: You will parent the same way I would in this situation.

Need: To know that he loves me and is listening to me.

Demand: Read this parenting book I gave you.

Expectation: We will be changing our parenting approaches at the same time, at the same pace.

Need: To feel supported as I make this big parenting change that is hard for me personally.

2. FIND OUT WHY THIS MATTERS TO YOU

As in our work with our children, the *why* is the most crucial step. It can be done without asking anything of our partner, without them being on the same page or pursuing this philosophy in any way. By digging deeply into your why, you are preparing yourself to take care of your own needs without generating expectations or making any demands. You are laying the groundwork for transformative conversations with your partner that will feel very different from the battles you may have had in the past. Supported by your deep why, you will know what actually matters to you, and you can move toward it with confidence.

Let's take one of the examples above and see how we can move from a demand to a need.

Demand: Let our child eat in his room instead of at the dinner table

Why does it matter that your partner let this kid eat in his room?

Because he is miserable at the table. This is a demand that's clearly too hard for him, which is why he keeps screaming at us, which just makes my partner mad at him.

(Be prepared that your initial answers will be all about your child, your spouse, projections, and other people. This is normal. It is hard to find yourself in this swirl of kids, co-parenting, and family dynamics. Be gentle and patient. You will get there if you keep asking the right question.)

Why does it matter that this makes your partner mad?

This matters because we're all overstimulated and tired after a long day, which makes it hard to communicate and be flexible and creative. When my partner gets mad, I get protective of our kids, so it's harder to stay aligned in our partnership. When my partner gets mad, he gets more rigid and inflexible and is more likely to insist on everyone staying at the table.

Why does it matter that I'm finding it hard to stay aligned?

I want to be on the same page as my partner, and I want him to do what I would do in that situation. *Ah-ha! The positive expectation that you have for your partner.* (Reminder, we are going to let this expectation go.)

Why does it matter that he does what you would do?

Because it is so vulnerable to be changing so much as a parent, and it would be less vulnerable if we were at the same place as we change. Because I want to trust him and to have him trust me. Because I'm scared that he isn't listening to me and doesn't care what I think. Because if he isn't listening to me, I'm scared that he doesn't really love me. *Oh. Now we got there. That's a need.*

Is your stomach clenching? Do you feel tears brimming? This is the real stuff, the lurking fears that drive us to insist that our partner do dinners in the exact same way as we would. Do you love me? Do you trust me? Are you listening? Do you care?

A discussion about where our child eats his dinner cannot hold these deep needs, though they are lurking everywhere. Our partner also cannot respond to this need if it is not expressed. They have their own deep needs. To have the real conversation about the deep needs, rather than the surface fight about who eats where, is the life-changing magic of low-demand parenting.

We shift our attention from the demands and expectations to listening and loving. The belief embedded in low-demand parenting is that we can be met and loved at the place of our deep need without asking our partner to meet our expectation or fulfill our demand. We can be loved, listened to, and trusted, no matter what happens with our child. But before you demand that your partner listen to you, you will instead work on your own listening posture. You will model the kind of empathetic listening that your partner truly needs. Not necessarily how you would want to be listened to, but how your partner wants to be listened to.

* * *

3. LISTEN TO YOUR PARTNER

Be careful of demands that arise even in the listening. At first, I pursued listening to my husband like a tiger stalking his prey. I had a topic I wanted to discuss, and I wanted to know exactly what was going on for my husband.

For us, it was screen-time. I could tell he was prickly about the decision to drop our boundaries and allow them to self-regulate with screens. I saw the shadow fall over his eyes every time he found one of our boys immersed in a video game. So I waited for a quiet moment and pounced with my questions. I wanted him to do the deep work on why this mattered, and I wanted him to do it now. Can you start to see all the demands I was heaping onto this situation?

- Talk now
- Talk for a long stretch
- Answer my questions
- All my questions
- Do your deep work
- Do your deep work right now
- Right in front of me
- Tell me about the deep work

- Right now.

Turned out that my pouncing tiger strategy didn't yield the result I wanted. If my deep why was to answer the questions, "Do you trust me? Do you love me?" then seeing him shut down before my barrage of questions didn't help either of us. It reinforced my belief that he didn't trust me and wasn't willing to do the work. That I was alone and couldn't trust him. But nothing could be farther from the truth. My demand factory led me astray, but genuine listening led me home.

Genuine listening

I considered the category of "meaningful communication" that I developed for my children. It was clear that Brian was not ready to have a face-to-face, intense, question-style conversation about his deep needs related to our kids' screen-time. But could I gently and compassionately observe my husband to find out what meaningful communication he was offering?

I observed that his eyes looked sad when he saw our kids playing games on their tablets, but I also noticed that he didn't overtly challenge them or tell them to get off. I could not control his emotions or make this less painful for him. But I could recognize his effort and accomplishment to tolerate this massive change in our family dynamic. I could give him space to arrive at his own destination in his own time.

Gentle curiosity

Once you know your true why, and you are ready to listen in the way your partner is ready to communicate, then you may try setting up a conversation with the stated goal simply to hear your partner's concerns. Give them free rein to state all the things that they are thinking, all the things that they are worried about, everything that they want to say. You may not ask any questions at all. You may allow silence and gentle curiosity to be invitation enough.

The opening to the conversation may sound like this: "I've

noticed that dinnertimes are stressful for all of us, and I'd love to hear more about your experience. I don't have an agenda. I have some preliminary ideas, but I don't want to go there yet. I just want to listen to what's hard about dinnertime for you. Are you open to that conversation? Maybe tomorrow night when the kids are in bed?"

Brian needs substantial lead time to think through my questions and even one day might not be enough processing time for a challenging topic. It's ok to float something and then wait a while to discuss it.

Slowing down

After all, slowing down is an important part of the process. We are often in a hurry to solve things because it feels so impossible, and something needs to *change!* Like *yesterday!* But Brian and I have found over and over that real change takes its own time, and being truly connected and aligned with another human is slow work. Urgency makes us skip steps and jump to solutions. We typically short-change the listening step.

So, take slow breaths, remember how long it took you to get into this situation and envision a path leading out of it. It may look long, and it will feel slow, but it is progress. You are walking in the right direction. To go there with a partner is worth it. It's ok to slow down and go together.

What do you do with your partner's concerns?

What happens with all the things your partner just shared?

Do you need to agree with these concerns? No.

Do you need to believe that they are real? No, you don't.

Is it your job to solve these problems? No, it's not.

Here's what you do right now: You do need to respect that these concerns are real *for them* and remember that it takes real courage and trust to share our true concerns. Your partner is loving you with their trust.

What you can do is repeat back what you've heard. "Am I hearing this right? It sounds like you are saying..." You may also ask, "Is there anything else?" Or, "Would you like more time to think about it? We can come back to this." The point is that you want to stay in the listening step until you've heard everything they have to say, and you've absorbed it.

We've had times when just the listening takes weeks. So, what do we do while we are just listening? I proactively drop as many demands as I can. All those other demands you listed for your partner that are not your top priority get dropped.

This doesn't mean that none of those things will happen, or that it all falls on you. It means that you proactively shift your expectations to focus on what matters most (the dinner table situation and your need to feel loved and listened to). Meanwhile, you also drop demands for your child.

The fastest way to get your partner on board with low-demand parenting is for them to experience the freedom of a low-demand partnership with you.

Let them off the hook. Let yourself off the hook. Let your child off the hook. Lower the bar. Let things go. The fastest way to turn them off from low-demand parenting is to ratchet up expectations, pushing them close to burnout.

4. STATE YOUR WHY AND YOUR NEEDS

Remember your deep why? The thing that made tears prickle and your stomach clench. You get to name that thing with your partner—*after* you've heard everything they have to say on the subject. *After* you have done deep, patient, gentle, curious listening, and they feel fully heard.

For some people, the waiting and the listening will be the hard part. You want to jump to your concerns and your ideas. You're bursting with things to say and getting peace with listening will be your big hurdle.

For other people, it is more natural to fall silent and listen. Owning your own experience and perspective is what's tricky. You may be petrified to say "I am scared you're not going to listen to me. I'm scared that means you don't love me" out loud, in front of your partner.

Still others will struggle with the faith that it is worth it, that any listening or speaking will produce meaningful change, that there is any way out of the awful place you are in right now.

Perhaps you are reading this list and thinking that your challenge is something totally different. The truth is that we will all have our unique struggles with owning our why and stating our needs.

This is a very vulnerable step for many of us because of our past stories around being heard and respected and valued as we share our deep selves, because it requires trust and intimacy and courage, and because we have to slow down and release our beloved solutions and instead stay with our needs.

For me, sharing vulnerably is hard because I fear the conflict of bringing my needs forward. It feels easier to pretend I have no needs, that I can seamlessly blend into the needs of the family, that I am happy if everyone else is happy. But that is not true. In fact, my deep needs broil in my stomach and come forward in my dreams. My body and my subconscious are not happy with my conscious brain's decision to be need-free.

This is a place to dig deeply with your trained professional—a therapist, a counselor, a coach, a psychiatrist, or even with a really wonderful friend. If you do not have a trained professional on your team, I believe that you deserve such a person in your corner, and that you are worthy of the investment it would take to find someone just for you. Doing the work you are doing is so hard. My hope for you is that you will be deeply supported along the way.

With a trained therapist, you may dig into the inner child who is terrified right now. You may process old trauma with your first family, or past experiences with this partner or others that are influencing how you show up with your why and your needs. If you do not have a trained professional right now, and you are struggling to bring your needs forward, you may want to journal on these questions:

- What emotion do I feel when I imagine sharing my deep why and my needs with my partner?

- Where do I feel this emotion in my body?

- Are there words or phrases that go along with it?

- Whose voice is speaking those words? Mine? Someone else's?

- What do I need to feel supported enough to share?

When you are ready, you may share these things openly with your partner. Sharing your deep why comes after you've already heard your partner's deep why.

As we moved through our journey related to the kids' screen-time, after deep listening to all my husband's concerns, I shared my deep why for letting the limits go. I told him that I was convinced that Michael needed full access to screen-time to reduce his threat response, and screen-time allowed me to keep the other two safely and independently occupied while Michael was aggressively dys-regulated for long and frequent periods of time.

We sat with my deep why—it was essential for regulation for Michael and helped keep the other kids safe—and his true concerns. He didn't have to solve this for me. He didn't have to agree with me. He didn't have to believe me. He just had to trust that I believed this, and that any solution needed to account for my belief.

Through this process, we saw the same situation through one another's eyes. We didn't come at it from a place of problem-solving, which might have led to dueling solutions to the same problem. Instead, by sharing and respecting one another's deep why, we were in a position to come up with solutions that would work for us all. Our metaphor for this posture became "sitting on the same couch." We would each have our own spot on the couch, but we were sitting next to one another, looking at the same situation.

Being "on the same page" was too restricting. Sometimes, we each had our own story, and each story took up its own page. But we could share our stories side by side on our metaphorical couch.

Stating our needs is an affirmation of our full humanity and our right to exist, which is a direct challenge to the forces that keep the status quo.

For those who are mothers, this is particularly important, as patriarchy and capitalism would prefer we remain blank canvases, free of pesky needs, ready to serve at all times. For those who are fathers, the patriarchy says, "Don't look deep inside, don't slow down, don't have feelings, just keep producing." Truthfully, we all feel these dual pressures, regardless of the roles we are socialized into. For all parents, the world says our labor is "free," our needs do not exist, and even if they do, they do not deserve institutional support.

I believe we are worthy of experiencing our full humanity, our full range of needs, and that we deserve vast and rich levels of support. Keep in mind that having needs and sharing them openly is an incredibly counter-cultural move. As you press against our society's negation of parental needs, you may feel this impacting your particular partnership. Know that it is not just you, not just your partner. Like other "isms", this is system-wide and acting in particular ways on you and your partner.

Declaring that we do not just exist to serve, or do not just exist to produce, challenges the status quo. It is a radically self-affirming act and a beautiful expression of your inherent dignity.

5. WORK PROACTIVELY TO DROP DEMANDS

Once you've named demands, identified your true why, listened deeply, and shared vulnerably, now you are ready to begin to drop demands in ways that will be life-giving for your partnership.

What demands can you proactively drop for one another? How can you drop these demands in ways that align with your priorities in the next season? If your priority is to support your struggling child into a season of greater stability, what demands can you drop for one another that make greater room for that?

Examples of demands we dropped for each other:

- Dishes (paper plates for a season)

- Cleaning (hired a professional cleaning team for a season, lived with a less clean house for a season)

- Healthy or home-cooked food (premade smoothies, Eggo waffles, cheese and crackers, PBJs were our dinners for a season)

- Meaningful conversation in the evenings (some nights I just needed to not talk; some nights Brian needed to jump straight into work)

- Agreeing on a path forward for the kids (more below).

Let's say that healthy or home-cooked food was a top priority for my husband, but I could not meet that demand. Then we would proactively come up with a creative solution to meet that priority without asking me to do anything differently. Perhaps there is a paid meal delivery service, or this would be a chance to reach out to the local community for a meal train (when people sign up to drop off food). Perhaps this is a time to switch cooking roles so that my husband, who cares most about food, would also be doing the cooking.

In our case, my husband was not able to take on the main cooking role, but he was able to cook a few quick meals to satisfy him on nights when all I could do was fall into bed. I agreed to stock the ingredients for those meals, which was not difficult for me.

We also proactively dropped the demand that we would agree on a path forward for the kids. My husband's top priority was stability for the children and reducing overwhelm for him. So, he proactively gave me permission to move forward with the low-demand approach, even though he wasn't able to invest highly in the process.

This worked for me. I agreed on the priority of stability for the kids, and I was able to drop my demand that he join equally in the process of discerning and dropping demands. I would take this on for the family if he would back me up as fully as he was able. I would also drop my demand that he always feel happy about my choices (it turns out you can't make someone feel something), but I asked that he not blame me or take his anger out on me.

Dropping demands felt a lot like asking for and giving permission. I dropped my internal demand to make only successful decisions and gave myself permission to mess up and learn from my mistakes. I proactively communicated this choice to Brian and asked for permission to fail on specific decisions without him calling the whole low-demand approach into question.

I realized that I could own the decision-making, take risks, and mess up, as long as I knew he was with me emotionally and would not blame me.

Brian realized that he could let me take the lead, knowing that I would listen to his feedback without judgment whenever he chose to share it, just as I had already. Even though we had countless examples of times I ignored his point of view, times he blamed me for making mistakes or took his anger out on me, we were able to communicate our needs and make a change.

It is never too late to try communicating in a new way. It is never too late to try a low-demand, low judgment, high communication, high compassion approach.

Let's take the dinner table example and explore how we approached this step, knowing that the particulars of your family will take your solutions in very different directions. This is truly a system, a process, a method. It won't work to copy our solutions because you will skip the steps of digging into your deep why, listening to your partner and working collaboratively to drop demands. Nonetheless, we all need to see this process in action to truly get it. So here's how we approached the family dinner table.

Dinner

Demand: Let our child eat in his room instead of at the dinner table.

Expectation: You will parent the same way I would in this situation.

Need: To know that he loves me and is listening to me.

Listening step: Dinner was feeling stressful and chaotic for everyone. It was hard for Brian to get home for dinner, and then to have to enter immediately into the most difficult time of day when he was exhausted and having trouble transitioning into the home environment. I was tired and acted mad at everyone. It was incredibly difficult for me to deliver one simultaneous eating experience with food that everyone would eat, all hot, all at the same time. Nonetheless, we knew that a family dinner where we sit together and talk is a hallmark of "good parenthood." Particular to us, we enjoy laughing with and talking to our kids, and both wished we had more group opportunities to do that.

Dropped demands: We dropped the "Family Dinner" demand. We moved the kids' meal to earlier, before Brian got home, and let them each eat on their own, which was a much better fit for their sensory profiles and eating needs. By dropping our screen-time limits, they were often each relaxing watching a show or playing a video game together around dinnertime.

Some nights I made an adult meal which we could some nights sit and eat together. I dropped the demand that Brian celebrate my cooking. If the food mattered to me, I would let him know that I worked hard on it so he could praise me. Brian had a little downtime to change out of his work clothes and transition into parenting. He and the kids then got to interact over more exciting activities like wrestling, building obstacle courses, running races outside, and playing board games. None of us missed the dinnertime stress.

6. GET CREATIVE IN TAKING CARE OF YOUR OWN NEEDS WITHOUT ASKING YOUR PARTNER TO DO ANYTHING DIFFERENTLY

At this point, you have listed demands, chosen a priority, listened to yourself to find your why, and listened to your partner to learn as much as you can. Then you worked together to drop demands of each other (and yourselves). After the process, you are probably wondering what to do with all the rest of it...

What about all those demands I proactively dropped?

Do all these dropped demands for everyone else end up piling up on my doorstep?

Am I expected to do everything because other people are struggling? No, no way, nope.

This last step is where you become a warrior for your own needs. This is where you love yourself into thriving. This is when you insist (to yourself) that you too are worthy of the same amount of love and accommodation you readily pour out onto your children.

Here's the truth: You cannot keep taking care of others without taking care of yourself—or you will burn out.

In this step, you take care of your own needs without asking your partner (or your kids) to do anything differently. I love this step. I'm like a demand dropping ninja. I especially love dropping demands for myself and taking care of my own needs. Empowerment, here I come!

Demand dropping examples

- I have a need to talk about my children, my parenting method, and what I've learned in the process. My partner is maxed out on this line of conversation. My solution: Connect with other parents online! My Instagram community has solved this need for me without needing my husband or children to do anything differently. I also have one friend who I connect with over video chat. We leave one another long monologue videos, a style of communication and listening that works for both of us. This relieves the pressure of me needing to info dump all of this on Brian.

- Brian is often working in the evenings and is not able to connect with me. I don't want to be disappointed on these nights when he retreats to his office to work and I am left alone. So I reserve a TV show that I only watch when he is too busy to connect. I look forward to the nights when he is too busy to hang out because I have a whole community of characters ready to step in. I also always have an engrossing novel to escape to, for nights when I just want to fall into bed.

- I need silence. I need the chance to sit in silence in my own house. This literally never happens during the day and can lead to resentment. So, I started going to bed earlier and getting up earlier than my earliest-riser (which is really darn early). I naturally wake up happy and feel my best first thing in the morning, so this system works for me. My husband is naturally a night-owl, and he would enjoy having our meaningful conversations later in the evening. This turns my brain on when I want to be winding down. I communicated this need, and through trial and error, we found a sweet spot window for conversation—late enough that he's getting a second wind, early enough that I can still go to bed early.

- I feel lonely and grumpy when I am cleaning, so I dropped the demand that I clean alone by making up personalities for my appliances. This works for my vibrant imagination (I easily created imaginary friends as a child too). My washing machine and dryer, dish washer, and robotic vacuum have become my "staff," and when they are working, I feel connected and less grumpy. It all happens in my mind, but it is still real. Plus, I can boss my staff around all I want, and they never have a meltdown.

- Folding laundry is my least favorite part of the process, and then I noticed resentment when my kids or spouse would riffle through their drawers, disrupting all my hard folding work. I also felt burdened that this responsibility consistently fell on me. It became impossible to give instructions to my kids about where to find their clothes as clothes could be anywhere—in the drawers in their rooms, folded in their baskets in the laundry area, or unfolded but clean, awaiting this dreaded task. Folding laundry and putting it away in the right places was too much of a demand for me. Maintaining folded laundry was too much of a demand for my family. Finding clothes spread in multiple locations was too much of a demand for everyone. I did a big drop by getting rid of kid dressers and keeping all our clothes in the laundry room. Now I toss clothes into the right kid's basket, and they can riffle through to their heart's content. We'd already dropped demands around wearing anything that might require hanging or could look "wrinkly," so this low-demand system works for us and our clothes.

Where we are now

We've been practicing this new way of co-parenting for over a year, and it has changed us significantly. I gave Brian his own time to adjust to the concept of low-demand parenting, without forcing him to be on the same page as me or to move through it in the same pacing as me. I took the lead, and he agreed to follow in his own way, in his own time. He followed through on his end of that bargain, without blaming me or second guessing the whole approach when things get hard.

My trust in myself and in Brian has increased, because I've realized that if I'm not scared that he will undercut me or blame me for mistakes, I can be brave, bold, and courageous. If I'm not scared of messing up, of being a "bad parent," or of losing my partner's love, I feel limitless. Without fear, I am free.

Brian needed to see that this new system was working to get fully on board, so he spent the first few months quietly watching and waiting. He practiced patience and was observant, like the talented scientist he is. He looked for evidence and tested the hypothesis. In the end, the data spoke clearly. In the process, he found that he had more natural freedom and flexibility in him than he even knew. His joyful nature and go-with-the-flow attitude flourished in our low-demand household, much more so than in previous iterations that required exacting parenting to ever get it all right.

Navigating all the accommodations I was making for the children was a challenge. I held the details of those accommodations in my head, and at first, it was difficult to download all he needed to know to step in. But over time, as we stopped dropping demands in the moment and got more proactive, we had fewer instances when we needed to rapidly align. Once we found a system that worked, like always taking two cars anytime the whole family tried a shared outing, then we would give it a name and use it over and over.

Our instincts have changed for one another. When things get hard, we look first at what demands are challenging for one or the other of us. Our first instinct is to lower the bar for success for ourselves, to take care of our own needs. We move much more quickly to identifying our adult need that is sitting at the root of a particular demand, and we have tested strategies to get our own needs met. There's humor and acceptance now, the kind of understanding that flows in a relationship, back and forth, back and forth.

Ultimately, we could not offer freedom and acceptance to each other, or our children, until we gave it to ourselves. Self-acceptance is the key to unlock the whole low-demand parenting approach. When we surround our own vulnerabilities and needs with compassion and acceptance, we have a well of grace to extend that same acceptance to our partner. When we feel empowered to meet our own needs without asking anyone else to do anything differently, we can accept the limits and boundaries of another without threat or shame. When we partner in co-parenting with acceptance, we have a true gift to offer our children. We cannot give them what we do not have for ourselves. We're only at the start of our journey, but this is a path we can walk for years. Grace only deepens and grows richer. Understanding and acceptance expand.

It turns out that letting things go for our kids was only the first step. The journey is truly a journey of love.

Chapter Twelve

Toward a Thriving Future

SQUARE PEGS IN A ROUND HOLE WORLD

I gave birth to square pegs. They never fit the milestones in the baby books or matched the infants and toddlers I saw in my friends' growing families. I had square pegs in a round hole world. What could I do?

I was very prepared for round pegs. I had done everything just right, exactly right. I read the baby books and took the birthing classes. I hired a Doula and made a birth plan. I was certain that I would be smooth and round, a perfect Mother. A round hole, ready to receive my round pegs.

Square pegs can only fit into round holes if they shave off most of who they are. Unfortunately, I knew just how to do this. This was my unique area of expertise. I had been shaving off parts of myself all the years of my life. When my babies were young, I didn't know yet that I was an undiagnosed autistic mother raising autistic children. All I knew was how to hustle, how to work harder than everyone else in order to be like everyone else, how to ignore the knowledge that I was different and instead plaster on a big smile and a Band-Aid, whittling, whittling, whittling away the Different until I was just the same.

I was a square peg who believed she was round.

But into the world my children arrived, perfectly shaped, perfectly square. Three square pegs in four short years.

I loved them so fiercely.

I never wanted them to change who they were, and yet we teach our children most by our example, by the way we choose to live, and I couldn't help it—I was teaching them to shave off their pointy corners and to change their distinctive shape. I was showing them all I knew to do—the way to become round.

With my oldest son, he dutifully followed. Like me, he became obsessed with the rules. If we always follow the rules, we will be safe. And he didn't just follow the rules, he took everything over the top. When he decided to be on time to elementary school, we ended up sitting in the parking lot for 20 minutes before the doors opened, so that he could be the very first person inside. He screamed and stomped his feet and shook with anxiety desperate to get into the car so he could be early for being early.

That's the problem with square pegs who shave off parts of themselves to become round. It's impossible to get the shape exactly right. And it is also impossible to hide the scars.

My second square peg took the opposite path. If there was a rule, he broke it. If there was a boundary, he crossed it. He was fierce and full and self-determined and strong and square. And no amount of whittling would change his shape. When I brought out my tools to carve him into a circle he brought out his tools and battled me. A warrior of independence.

Battling my son destroyed me. Or I should say it destroyed the old me. After denying myself for so long I busted out of my round hole mold in order to be reborn in my proper shape and to take up my mantle as a square mother in a round hole world.

Busting out of my round mold and growing corners again was intensely painful. Much like childbirth, creating new life also leaves scars. It changes you. I would be scarred either way.

We burned out on this round world and these whittling tools and the pain of squeezing into a shape that never ever had us in mind. At first, I could only see failure, a failure of a mom, but that too broke down. It all had to break.

To all the world it looked like a failure. All the markers of what good moms do were completely gone, and I believed that I had failed. But one day a friend suggested an alternative narrative, what if I wasn't breaking down? What if I was breaking free? What if letting everything fall away was a kind of freedom, a release of long-held dreams that were never the right shape for me or my family? To accept my children, I needed to accept myself. Radical self-acceptance is necessary to accept my children and create a world where they can flourish.

The more I accept myself—autistic, a square peg, different, and just right—the better I can form a brave new life for my family.

I am a square peg. My old shape broke apart and my new square self was reborn. I am a square peg mom, wildly accepting, free to make up my own rules, to shape my own world. A world where my little square pegs will not shave off their corners or pretend to be what they are not for anyone.

"I am remaking the world" becomes my new refrain. As we accept ourselves, we create a world together where difference is celebrated and specific support needs arise without shame. We are our own support group, a safe place to fumble through and learn together. Our family is a new family. Our world, a new world. As we are reborn, we transform our world.

LIVING IN-BETWEEN

As my family heals, the challenges still come. Michael still erupts every day, sending all of us to a different floor of the house while he stomps and screams and calms down. Owen still has panic attacks and cannot sit at the table or listen to someone chew. We're learning to live in the in between. It's not like being in crisis, and it's not "all better." It is staying curious and open when my child wants to move to absolutes. It's co-regulating and listening and empathizing and co-regulating and naming feelings and solving problems and co-regulating, every time, every day. I know now that these struggles are harder and come more frequently for parents of neurodivergent kids. This is our normal. We count "good days" or "hours since the last meltdown." We track medication changes and keep notebooks full of journal entries.

The hardest part for me is the not-solving. The living-with. Adapting my identity and capacity to account for the exhausting everyday reality of parenting in my shoes. We've been through so many acute crises that it feels easier to go into crisis mode than to live with the uncertainty of the long haul. I want to move quickly to a solution, even if it involves a crisis-style intervention, rather than watching and waiting and trusting that I will have enough for today, and tomorrow, and the daily difficulties to come.

TRANSFORMED ME

The biggest transformation takes place inside me. As I release my hold over these children, I begin to align with them differently. When it was my job to feed them certain foods, to stimulate them with wholesome activities, to engage them in meaningful conversation, and to ensure they represented me well in the world, I was always hustling. I could not rest, and the job was never done. I was always pushing them to be better than they were. And they resented me for it. As I begin to drop demands and accept the place we are in over the dream I have of where we ought to be headed, I notice our relationship transform. I am no longer dreaming of things being different. I dream of standing with these kids, no matter what they face, no matter how long it takes, no matter what. I am on their side, always.

The more I release expectations, the more our trust grows. One afternoon, in what looks like the lead up to a meltdown, Michael stomps down the hallway, banging every door he passes. But then he stops, turns, and runs back to hide under a blanket right by my side. Little by little, he wiggles until he is on my lap, blanket still over his head. He wallows into my chest, and I murmur, "You're doing your best, Michael, always." His head smushed into the crook of my elbow, I hear a tiny voice, "I love you, Mommy."

As I look forward, I dream of stepping even farther into advocacy for my children. Michael still struggles to wear shoes, and dog walkers on our block regularly stop and ask him where his shoes are. I am always perplexed at why strangers are so invested in my child's shoe choice, but I wave at them with a friendly smile and call out, "He's ok the way he is." The message is about more than what's not on his feet. He's ok standing there playing without shoes. He's ok loving the squish of socks on wet grass. He's ok not waiting even

30 seconds to get outside to play. I want to call it out to the whole world, "He's ok the way he is. We're ok the way we are."

DREAMING NEW DREAMS

I dreamed of calm, quiet dinners, of well-behaved children, of crafting, of glowing parent-teacher conferences. I dreamed of staying on the path, of having an easy time of it. I dreamed of my children having loads of friends, of after school activities like gymnastics and violin lessons. I dreamed of family bike rides, and siblings who are best friends. My old dreams died, one after another. And I grieved every one. Those were good dreams, and I know why I held on to them for so long. I believed that keeping the dream alive helped me to cope and gave me something to aim for. It turns out, they were my cage. A dreamer, I could not see the life before my eyes.

I watched other families living my dreams, knowing it was possible, and fantasizing about being someone else, someone who could make my dreams come true. If I was a different mom, if I had different kids, if I had a different spouse, then I could have the life of my dreams. I always asked, "What am I doing wrong?" I could not see that we were doing something powerfully right.

My dreams invoked streams of judgment over the life I actually lived. Every dream was laced with negation, distancing me from the goodness before my eyes. Our dinners were calm and quiet, yes, but they happened with each child in front of their own screen, and that was not the dream. My children can self-advocate, can ask for what they need, can name hidden realities others would rather ignore, but they do not say "please" and "thank you" or "yes ma'am" on cue. So, are they still well-behaved children? They will rip every prescribed Valentine's craft project into itty bitty pieces, but they can create elaborate houses in Minecraft, complete with rooms decorated in my favorite colors where I can come and stay when I visit. Our after-school activities are therapies, not gymnastics and violin. My dreams kept me far off, standing at a distance from my own life, always judging and finding it lacking.

But those dreams never saw me or my children anyway. In those dreams, Mom is small and silent and empty, fulfilled in shuttling her kids from one activity to another, in prompting them to "ask nicely," in keeping her house clean and tidy and her husband happy. In these dreams, Dad is rarely even in view. In these dreams, children are small and silent and empty too. We are all empty, ready to be filled with culturally approved aspirations of being good, being nice, not rocking the boat, not challenging the system.

When my old dreams died and fertilized the soil, it made rich loam for fresh dreams to take root, dreams long buried, ready to finally spring to life. We are creating a new world, these children and I. I dream that a new world might be born in us, radically self-accepting. I dream of not asking the world to make room for us, but declaring that we are already here, that we already deserve the space we take up.

LOW-DEMAND FUTURE

As my children grow and the challenges they face grow more complex, the wisdom gained from low-demand parenting feels all the more valuable. The skills of listening and sharing will serve us as hormones and social worlds tip our world on its axis. My low-demand partnership with my spouse enables us to communicate openly and share our needs, even as I move into a new season as a writer. And yet, no one knows what the future holds, and so I hold even this approach with low-demand hands. If my children require something different, I will learn, I will adapt, I will respond. After all, the greatest transformation has happened inside of me. By giving up adult power over children and giving up on the proscribed, socially-acceptable dreams, I step into total freedom. As long as my kids and I are aligned and connected, the journey can take us where it will. My children can change radically, and I will be here for them.

Resources

Pages marked with ★ are available to download from www.jkp.com/catalogue/book/9781839977688

DAY-FLOW WORKSHEET

What big demands structure your child's routines? Where do you see resistance or difficulty?

Waking

....
....

Breakfast eating

....
....

Playing/learning

....
....

Eating

....
....

Playing/learning

....
....

Eating

....
....

Bedtime

....
....

Define the Demand (Step 1) Worksheet

Name the big demand

....

Name the tiny demands

1. What must be stopped in order to meet the expectation?

....

....

2. How must it be stopped to meet the expectation?

....

....

3. When does this expectation need to happen?

....

....

4. How quickly must it happen?

....

....

5. By a certain time?

....

....

6. Will it be a race, and does the child need to be first?

....

....

7. What must happen before or after?

....

....

8. Where must it happen?

....

....

9. In a certain position?

....

....

10. With specific items?

....

....

11. What order must it be done in?

....

....

12. Quietly?

....

....

13. Who else is there at the same time?

....

....

14. Alone or with help?

....

....

15. Which helper?

....

....

16. With spoken words?

....

....

17. With specific spoken words?

....

....

18. With listening to spoken words?

....

....

19. With listening to specific spoken words?

....

....

20. What happens once the expectation is done?

....

....

DEMAND DROPPING WORKSHEET

1. What demand needs to be dropped?

....

....

2. Why does this demand matter to me? (And why does that matter? And why does that matter?...)

....

....

....

....

What do I hope they will learn by letting this go?

....

....

What is it about (expectation/demand/hope) that (positive result you want to happen)?

....

....

3. What does your child think about this demand?

Prep your statements:

I wonder if ....

....

I'm curious about ....

....

I have a guess that it's hard when ....

....

I'm not sure if I am getting this right ....

....

I'm thinking that ....

....

For me, I notice ....

....

4. Work proactively and work in batches

Can you make one decision that eases your daily life? Can you communicate it to your children and your people?

....

....

....

....

5. Get creative in taking care of your own needs, without asking your child to do anything differently!

....

....

....

....

6. Create house rules

....

....

....

....

DOCUMENT SCREEN-TIME LEARNING

Social/emotional learning:

....

....

....

....

Relational learning:

....

....

....

....

Academic learning:

....

....

....

....

Executive functioning learning:

....

....

....

....

★

SCRIPTS

For telling a casual observer who seems judgy

Don't bother. Shrug, say "This is what works for us," and move on.

For telling a casual acquaintance who genuinely wants to know

I use a specific parenting method that means I meet him where he's at and focus on connection over expectations.

For explaining to a grandparent, close friend, etc

I am working to intentionally create a lifestyle that calms my child, so they can thrive. The key to calming them is lowering what I ask of them proactively, in advance. Ironically, by asking less, I find my child is able to do more because they are calm and steady. This also creates a family culture of trust and connection, which I am prioritizing over everything else.

For explaining to a caregiver, therapist, or someone who will be interacting with your child

We use a pretty specific caregiving method for this child. It's very effective for all sorts of kids, but especially uniquely wired kids surviving a world not made for them. My kiddo has [share more about any specific diagnoses or traits you think are important]. So, to keep their brain–body system calm and steady, we use a low-demand approach. We lower what we ask of this child as much as possible and focus on connection. Here are some simple ways to join us in this strategy:

★

When you're interacting, use as few words as possible, relax your shoulders, smile and speak slowly. We do not make them... (tell them your big drops).

AFFIRMATIONS FOR PARENTS OF UNIQUELY WIRED KIDS

1. I can let this go.

Power battles with your kid are not where you want to be. If you say, "It's brush teeth time!" and they scream "NO!", it's ok to let it go. Tomorrow, you may try again or you may try differently. It is ok to let things go and to take things one at a time. It does not make you a bad parent, does not make you permissive, will not make things harder down the road.

2. I am the adult, but I do not have to be the boss.

You get to be the one who has the more developed brain and the more substantial life experience, who knows your life will not end if you release an expectation or feel disappointment. It's highly likely that your child does not know this yet, or cannot believe this in a moment of dysregulation.

3. I can always be creative. I can always be flexible.

These tools are always available to you. You can make it a game; you can become a character or an animal. You can pretend to lose. You can change the situation to make it easier on your child or on you.

4. I hold things loosely, while knowing what matters most.

You are capable of holding your plans and expectations loosely without giving up your whole life and your sanity. There's no need to play things forward, to imagine how much worse it could get. Instead, use your limited mental energy to stay focused on the one or two things that matter most. Perhaps today it is stability, connection, mental or bodily safety, or fun.

5. It's not personal. They don't mean it.

This is for all the parents who are blamed for the milk being too thick one morning or for the socks getting wet in the grass when the child chose not to wear shoes outside. This is for the times they scream "I hate you," "Shut up," and "I wish you weren't my mom." It's not personal, it's really not. They really do not believe that or mean that or wish that. It's ok to have selective memory here. It's ok to let it go.

6. This is a neurobiological disability, a brain difference.

Our differently wired children go into the fight or flight pathway in interactions we might perceive as being very small or unimportant. That does not negate the power of the brain–body experience that our child is having. This difference is disabling.

7. My child is having a really hard time.

The difficulty may look like defiant or deliberate behaviors, and you may hear or believe that these behaviors are in their control, but this is not true. Your child is experiencing a severe brain–body reaction that is really hard on them. They are suffering. When you meet their challenge with compassion, it will increase your child's sense of safety and connection.

8. We all do well when we can, and when we can't we give each other grace.

Rewards and punishments are not necessary to change behavior because we are all intrinsically motivated to do our best to please the people we love and to meet their expectations. We are already hard-wired to do this to the best of our ability. If we are not able to do well, it is because something is getting in our way. For you and for your child, step back and give grace when things are hard. Drop expectations and accept half-measures.

9. I do not need to have all the answers to get started, and it is never too late.

You do not need to know all your child's diagnoses or be a parenting expert to start down a new road. You can always make a change. It is never too late to learn and grow, and even adult children can benefit from a parent who learns how to connect with a low-demand relationship.

10. There are parents in the world who know what I am going through. I am not alone here.

Feeling misunderstood, judged, and alone is a toxic combination that so many parents can understand. You are not alone; many others can relate and empathize. No matter what you are facing today, you are not in this alone.

LOW-DEMAND COMMUNICATION PROMPTS

Practice your declarative language.

Declarative language is a statement or an observation that does not ask anything specific of the listener.

Declarative language will observe something about a situation, narrate something happening, or notice a fact your child may have missed. Declarative language is the opposite of imperative language—a question or a sentence that demands a response, whether a verbal response or an action (e.g., "It's time to stop your video" versus "I wonder how much time is left in your video").

I wonder if...

....

....

....

....

I'm curious about...

....

....

....

....

I have a guess that it's hard when...

....

....

....

....

★

I'm not sure if I am getting this right...

....

....

....

....

I'm thinking that...

....

....

....

....

For me, I notice... (state something true about yourself that may or may not be true for them)

....

....

....

....

NONVERBAL SUPPORT: STOP SLIDER

How to use this nonverbal support

As you start a conversation, place this "stop slider" down on the ground next to you. Start by affirming that whenever they are ready to be done, you can stop (point to Stop). You can even stop when they get close to being ready to stop (point to the feet closest to the stop sign). Say: "If you're ok to talk (point to the thumbs up), I'm curious about...(say what topic you want to hear more about)."

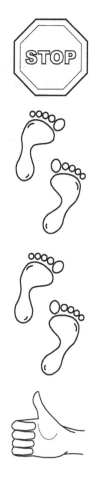

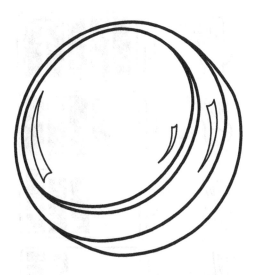

NONVERBAL SUPPORT: PANIC BUTTON

How to use this nonverbal support

When you are heading into an unfamiliar environment, especially with an adult in charge who is not you, print out and bring this support. Print your name and phone number on the back and show it to the adult in charge. Reinforce that if your child shows this image, the child wants them to call you immediately. Your child can fold it and put it in their pocket, and pull it out to communicate their need to leave without words.

I'M READY TO GO HOME

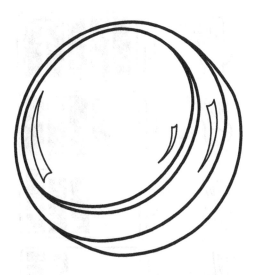

NONVERBAL SUPPORT: BATTERY PACK

How to use this nonverbal support

Post this at home and bring with you into unfamiliar or challenging environments to support your child in communicating their energy levels nonverbally. You can flash a hand and they can put up fingers to show their energy level. Decide in advance when you will leave (maybe one day you will leave at 2 and other days it will be at 3). Discuss how technology powers down when it gets too low, and that you want to leave with some energy left in their battery. Talk about ways they can recharge if they want to stay longer.

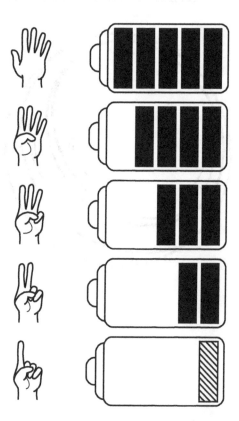

Further Reading

The Lazy Genius Way: Embrace What Matters, Ditch What Doesn't, and Get Stuff Done by Kendra Adachi

Not a parenting book. Just an incredible resource for figuring out what really matters and giving yourself permission to let things go. This book's motto is "Be a genius about the things that matter and lazy about the things that don't." And that is core to the low-demand parenting life.

Outside the Box: Rethinking ADD/ADHD in Children and Adults by Thomas E. Brown, PhD

This is a dense and powerful book for challenging old ideas of ADHD and embracing the science behind this brain difference. It conveys scientific information in simple terms that everyone can understand, while maintaining a complex portrait of what the evidence demonstrates about ADHD.

Brain-Body Parenting: How to Stop Managing Behavior and Start Raising Joyful, Resilient Kids by Mona Delahooke

You want someone who gets it, who has a PhD and pours over the latest brain science, and who is gentle, kind, and helpful. You've found her. Her name is Mona Delahooke and you are going to love this book and want to share it with all the grandparents.

Beyond Behaviors: Using Brain Science and Compassion to Understand and Solve Children's Behavioral Challenges by Mona Delahooke

This is Dr. Delahooke's first book, a manual for re-learning how to interpret your child's behaviors through the lens of neuroscience. She looks at the nervous system level of children's behavior and argues that all the punishments and rewards only elevate a child's stress and escalate troubling behaviors.

Raising Human Beings: Creating a Collaborative Partnership with Your Child by Ross W. Greene, PhD

This companion to *The Explosive Child* outlines the philosophy behind the parenting approach, including how this approach positively impacts your relationship to all your children, including neuro-typical ones.

The Explosive Child: A New Approach for Understanding and Parenting Easily Frustrated, Chronically Inflexible Children by Ross W. Greene, PhD

To go deeper into collaboration with your child, this is *The Book* to read. Low-demand parenting is very in line with the "plan C" piece of this method, but to learn all the steps to solve problems collaboratively and proactively, this book will walk you through every step.

Declarative Language Handbook: Using a Thoughtful Language Style to Help Kids with Social Learning Challenges Feel Competent, Connected, and Understood by Linda K. Murphy MS, CCC-SLP

This is a small and immanently instructive book, written by a speech language pathologist. It will help you transform your language with low-demand suggestions and tons of examples.

Burnout: The Secret to Unlocking the Stress Cycle by Emily Nagoski and Amelia Nagoski

So many parents arrive at caregiver burnout without having any idea how to release stress and move through emotions. *Burnout* is practical and understanding, written by neurodivergent sisters who have each experienced substantial burnout themselves.

Uniquely Human: A Different Way of Seeing Autism by Barry M. Prizant, PhD

This compassionate approach to autism outlines the basic theory of neurodiversity: Autism is not an illness; it is a new way to be human. I find it extremely helpful in understanding and celebrating the uniqueness of our autistic kids.

Differently Wired: Raising an Exceptional Child in a Conventional World by Deborah Reber

The founder of the website, podcast, and parenting community called Tilt Parenting, Debbie Reber is a leading voice for embracing neurodiversity and transforming the world for our uniquely wired kids. This book is honest and motivating, part memoir, part manifesto. It is a call to action to show up and change the world into a place where all can thrive.

PATHOLOGICAL DEMAND AVOIDANCE

The Family Experience of PDA: An Illustrated Guide to Pathological Demand Avoidance by Eliza Fricker

A quick read, easy to share with family members, and filled with whimsically true illustrations, this book is one I reach for most often.

The Teacher's Introduction to Pathological Demand Avoidance: Essential Strategies for the Classroom by Clare Truman

Though this book was written for teachers, we use these strategies every day in our home. Packed with practical advice, this is also a great book to share with therapists and caregivers. Essential reading for unschooling parents.

PDA North America

pdanorthamerica.com

This website is rich with resources for individuals and families living with Pathological Demand Avoidance in North America, led by professionals and PDA experts Laura Kerbey and Diane Gould. Find videos, webinar trainings and an annual conference, as well as a list of certified trained PDA trainers and parents.

PDA Society

pdasociety.org.uk

A global center for research, training, and support, the PDA Society is based in the U.K. This vast resource combines policy papers and training opportunities with advocacy and fundraising.

SCREEN-TIME

"Children's Screentime Guidelines Too Restrictive According to New Research"

In a new study, published in the journal *Child Development*, researchers from the Oxford Internet Institute and Cardiff University tested the recommendations of the American Academy of Pediatrics (AAP), which proposes a limit of one to two hours per day as good for the psychological wellbeing of young children. See https://www.ox.ac.uk/news/2017-12-14-children's-screen-time-guidelines-too-restrictive-according-new-research for a summary.

"The Kids Who Use Tech Seem to Be All Right"

Scientists at the University of Oxford published a study in *Nature Human Behaviour* showing that technology use has a nearly negligible effect on adolescent psychological well-being. "Technology use tilts the needle less than half a percent away from feeling emotionally sound. For context, eating potatoes is associated with nearly the same degree of effect and wearing glasses has a more negative impact on adolescent mental health." See www.scientificamerican.

com/article/the-kids-who-use-tech-seem-to-be-all-right for a summary.

The New Childhood: Raising Kids to Thrive in a Connected World by Jordan Shapiro

This book is a refreshing look at children's relationship with technology grounded in the latest research and free from fear. *The New Childhood* argues that technology is moving us toward a better future, that our children will have fresh models of global citizenship, and ways to connect and to exist in community.

Moral Combat: Why the War on Violent Video Games Is Wrong by Patrick Markey and Christopher Ferguson

These two scientific researchers look closely at the data on violent video games' influence on human behavior and mental health, and interweave their conclusions that there is no data to support many of the claims that these games have a negative impact with humor and conviction.

Acknowledgments

This project grows from a story of pain, the loss of all the systems I believed would support me and the breakdown of the old beliefs I held dear. Out of the rubble, we emerged with this low-demand parenting approach. But I never would have taken the first step without the B Team Facebook community, and especially the high-quality moderators who make that community what it is. Thank you, Zaidee and Heather, for pouring life into people in the pit, and for believing we all do well when we can, even when we can't believe it for ourselves.

I am also grateful to the Hope*Writers community, especially Emily P. Freeman, Brian Dixon, and Niki Hardy, who each taught me what I needed to know that move forward as a writer and fall deeper in love with the craft of words.

The caregivers who surrounded my family during our hardest moments will always have a special spot in my heart. Thank you, Becca Morris, for stepping in during a season when we needed you so badly. Your gentleness and joy are the greatest gift. Thank you to Laura Phoenix for the ways you've made my body a safe place to dwell, and to Brittany Weber for sitting with me through all my darkness. You are my favorite, Erin Heinz, and I am so glad you see me. To the amazing therapy team at Emerge Pediatric Therapy, we would be lost without you—especially Andrew, Jaclyn, Anna, and Nicole.

I want to thank my parents who fostered my intense, sensitive, and dynamic little spirit and raised me to be the person I am. Thank you for all the hours you listened to my stream of consciousness and watched my dance routines. Thank you for your own courageous choices to step off the mainstream parenting path. Thank you for loving me through all these changes and discoveries. You are incredible, and it's from your steady love that I am able to launch.

To my incredibly supportive wider family—Tom and Anne, thank you for cheering for me and being the greatest brother and sister I could want. You two inspire me to walk my own path, to laugh more, and to throw a big party, not a small one. Patti and Mark, for your fiercely supportive love, for the gift of writing time, and for all the ways large and small that you wrap me up in your love. Casey and Rachel, thank you for modeling gentle acceptance; thank you for hours of beach joy and for letting me make all the decisions.

To the people who never stop listening, never stop showing up, and who keep me laughing, walking, and celebrating: Charlene, Stephanie, Kristen, Ellie.

To my Monday night group, you've prayed me through every single step and believed I would find my way when I couldn't believe it. I am so glad we just keep showing up for each other.

To my husband Brian, you are the rock of my life, my safety net when I decide to fly high, and my favorite dance partner. I only hope I can be the woman I see in your eyes. I thank God for giving me this one precious life to love and live with you.

And to my children, when you read this one day, know that through every hard moment, I loved you more and more. I am so proud of you for having the courage to speak to me in the ways you knew how, for showing me your pain, and for trusting me to change the world for you to thrive. No matter what, no matter what, no matter what, I will always show up for you. Watching your life's journeys is the greatest joy I have ever known.

And to you, my readers, my fellow parents who are ready to change the world for your kids, I wish for you the knowledge that good parenting is a myth, that you are endlessly brave, and that our children are our true teachers.

About the Author

Amanda Diekman is an ordained Presbyterian pastor, spiritual director, coach, and autistic contemplative.

A dual graduate of Duke University with a master's in divinity, Amanda devoted her ministry career to relational organizations pursuing justice and equity, including leading the international Pilgrimage of Pain and Hope in Brazil, founding a bilingual congregation in the US, and serving as longstanding board chair with nonprofit Reality Ministries.

She lives in her favorite city in the world, Durham, NC, with her husband and three young ones. They live in the North Street Community, an intentional residential community with neighbors of all abilities.

She has been published extensively online, including at Her View from Home, Not An Autism Mom, PDA Parents, and the Mighty. You can find her writing online at www.amandadiekman.com and engage with her on Instagram @lowdemandamanda.